MW00572951

Dr Steve Morlidge

THE

(ILLUSTRATED)

LITTLE^BOOK

OF

OPERATIONAL

FORECASTING

A short introduction to the practice and
pitfalls of short term forecasting...

...and how to
increase its value to
the business

Matador
9 Priory Business Park,
Wistow Road, Kibworth Beauchamp,
Leicestershire. LE8 0RX
Tel: 0116 279 2299
Email: books@troubador.co.uk
Web: www.troubador.co.uk/matador
Twitter: @matadorbooks

ISBN 978 1789013 429

British Library Cataloguing in Publication Data.
A catalogue record for this book is available from the British Library.

Printed and bound by CPI Group (UK) Ltd, Croydon, CR0 4YY
Typeset in 9pt Adobe Garamond Pro by Troubador Publishing Ltd, Leicester, UK

Matador is an imprint of Troubador Publishing Ltd

CONTENTS

Preface   xi
How It Came About   xii
Format   xvi
Structure   xviii
Terminology   xxi
Disclaimer   xxii

1. The Purpose of Forecasting   1

What IS a forecast?   2
Forecasts are not the same as budgets or plans   4
Different kinds of forecast   6
All operational forecasting is based on the same principles   8
Why operational forecasting is important   10
The quality of forecasts matters...a lot   12
Forecasting is a (very) good investment   14
Forecasting is not compulsory   16

2. Understanding Demand — 19

Data Series are different - and it matters to forecasters — 20
Forecasting is not easy — 22
It is not possible to predict the future — 24
It is not easy to spot noise — 26
Types of Signal — 28
The buckets used to measure demand changes the
    characteristics of the data — 30
Characteristics of operational demand data — 32

3. Forecasting Methods — 35

The forecasting challenge — 36
Three ways to produce forecasts — 38
Forecasting by extrapolating from historic time series — 40
Forecasting using causal models — 42
Forecasting using judgement — 44
Three types of bias in judgemental forecasting — 46
The better the fit to history -
    (sometimes) the worse the forecast method — 48
How to avoid overfitting — 50
Sophisticated methods are
    (often) no better than simple ones — 52

The methods used in different
   software packages are not unique   54
The methods used in different
   software packages are not always correct   56
Autoselect algorithms do not
   always select the best forecasting method   58
Machine learning technology will not   60
eliminate the need for human input into forecasting   60
Combining forecasts produces better results   62

4. Understanding Forecast Performance   65

The measurement challenge   66
Conventional error metrics   68
Period errors are not meaningful   70
The denominator is not important   72
Value Added - the ultimate measure of forecast quality 74
Forecast Value Added (FVA) - the measure of the
   effectiveness of steps in the forecast process   76
Some demand series are more forecastable than others   78
Comparing to the naïve forecast error adjusts for
   forecastability   80

How to quantify the level of avoidable errors –
the limits of forecastability   82
Errors always increase over time   84
Allow for different lags when measuring the value
    added by forecasts   86
Bias and variation – two types of error   88
The different business impact of bias and variation   90
The causes of bias   92
The causes of variation   94
Conventional error metrics treat bias
    and variation in an inconsistent way   96
Forecasts do not need to be equally accurate across the
    horizon.   98
Sometimes a forecast is not a forecast   100
The best forecasts do not always have the lowest errors   102
It is not possible to compare forecast error across levels   104
Error levels cannot be compared and targeted   106
It is not impossible to benchmark forecast quality   108
It is not possible to measure the quality of long term
    forecasts   110
Forecastability does not describe how easy it is to
    forecast demand   112

5. Managing Forecast Performance   115

Forecast improvement is based on understanding error   116
Forecasting is not mandatory   118
The objective should not be to increase forecast accuracy 120
Forecasting does not always add value   122
Few things are unforecastable   124
Good forecasts don't always 'look right'   126
Reacting to noise makes things worse   128
Focussing on the biggest errors is not the best way
    to improve forecast quality   130
You can only measure and manage forecast errors trends 132
Improving short term forecasts is not always worthwhile 134
Judgemental forecasts are not always bad or alwaysgood 136
Consensus forecasting is not (necessarily) 'best practice' 138
Experts are (often) no better at forecasting than
    non-experts   140
The level of aggregation affects the ease of forecasting   142
When to use 'top down' and 'bottom up' forecasting methods 144
To disaggregate or aggregate?   146
Why we clean history and when to do it   148
Judgement and when to use it   150
More frequent re-forecasting is not (necessarily) better   152
Segment the product portfolio to get better results   154

Standard deviation is not the way to measure volatility   156
Better forecasts do not automatically
    generate business benefit   158
A business should always have 'one set of forecast
    numbers'   160
The forecast numbers do not always need to be the same   162
It doesn't matter who forecasters report to – providing...   164

Terminology   166
Calculating Value Added Metrics   172
Recommended Reading   174
Acknowledgements   176

PREFACE

This is a guidebook about short term Operational Forecasting – the sort that is done to determine how much product you need to source or how many people you need to draft in to meet customer demand.

My aim is to produce something that provides a useful introduction to operational forecasting for both practitioners and their bosses by filling in the gap that lies between a naïve 'common sense' intuitive grasp of the topic and the complex technicalities of mathematical forecasting techniques.

I think my background as a self-taught business orientated forecasting nerd with limited mathematical expertise who is not scared to tell it the way I see it puts me in a good position to fill this gap.
I have designed the book to be simple but not simplistic, using short and to the point learning points supported by clear graphics. It is technically sound and practical.

I hope it will create a common language to help people talk intelligently about forecasting and help stop people doing dumb stuff – which is where most of the potential for improvement lies. I hope it will help people design good forecast processes and informed software purchasing decisions. And I hope that it will in some small way help people realize that forecasting is important and that investing in people as well as software will generate enormous benefits for many businesses.

HOW IT CAME ABOUT

This is a book I had never intended to write but it was one that I felt needed to be written.

Just before I left Unilever after a career in Finance I designed and led a change initiative that aimed to replace traditional bureaucratic budgeting practices with more agile planning processes, based on the Beyond Budgeting model, that would enable businesses to better adapt to the world.

As part of this effort I chose to focus on improving forecasting, as I reckoned that only when people had a future orientated process that they could rely on would they let go of budgeting – however much they hated it.

As I did more and more research on this topic I came to realize that no-one in the finance community – inside or outside of Unilever – really understood business forecasting. And I included myself in this number despite having been responsible for forecasting for nearly 20 years.

What I learned on this journey eventually led to me writing my first book 'Future Ready', which is still the only book on the market covering this important topic.

In this work on business forecasting I drew heavily on the insights of academic and practitioners working to improve operational forecasting in the supply chain.

It shouldn't be surprising that so much energy and expertise is devoted to the challenge of forecasting demand since it provides the foundation upon which supply planning sits.

Typically, any business selling from stock will need to produce many thousands of forecasts very frequently, and the results have a direct and immediate bearing on the business. Get it wrong and you can either end up with too much stock that costs you a lot of money or too little which leads to disappointed customers and losing what is left of your fortune. And it is possible to do both at the same time in different parts of the product portfolio!

I came to develop an enormous respect for the expertise and professionalism of people working in this field, but before long I had an experience that was just as shocking and surprising to me as the realization that I had when I discovered how little I knew about business forecasting even after 20 years of practice. None of these really smart people could answer what I thought was a pretty obvious question: 'how do I know how good my forecast is?' The existence of this gaping hole in our knowledge intrigued and frustrated me in equal measure and so I set out to find the answer for myself.

My quest for an answer to this question ultimately led to me co-founding a software business, CatchBull, and over time I became an accidental expert on the topic, with a handful of academic publications to my name.

Naively, I assumed that selling this product would be easy, because the need and the business benefits were so obvious. Instead when I spoke to business people I found a blank wall of incomprehension. And I got a similar reaction from many academics and software suppliers I encountered.

What was going on?

What I slowly came to realize is that most people in the supply chain simply do not appreciate the nature of the challenge of forecasting demand at the very granular (detailed) level at which it takes place, and the scale of the benefits if you can get it right. My problem was that because I had immersed myself in the problem for years I had lost touch with my old ignorant self and I assumed that the professionals I spoke to would appreciate the nature of the challenge – and the opportunity – in the same way as me, which they clearly did not.

This was forcibly brought home to me in a conversation I had with the leader of the demand management process for a major multinational.

The conversation went something like this:

> Me: '…of course it simply isn't possible to forecast the future perfectly'
> Head of Demand Planning 'Why not?'
> Me: '……..' (stunned silence)

The reason why I had been rendered uncharacteristically mute was that it suddenly became clear to me that he and I had a completely different view of the world – of the reality of trying to anticipate future demand. And that I didn't know how to bridge the gap.

I believed – I would say I knew – that because the world is volatile, uncertain, complex and often ambiguous ('VUCA'), anticipating the future is difficult, and that there is an inherent limit to how accurate any forecast can be. As a result, I believe the only way to proceed is to do the best job you can of predicting the future but then, with humility, measure how successful you have been, learn and adjust your methods accordingly.

If, on the other hand, like my friend, you think the world is perfectly predictable, you must believe that there is a clockwork like mechanism hidden from our sight that governs what happens in the world. Forecasting therefore simply involves trying to discover and replicate the working of this cosmic machine where free will and chance play no part. If that is what you believe then producing good forecasts is purely a matter of building a sophisticated mathematical model, and errors are a purely a manifestation of our ignorance.

But even supply chain leaders who acknowledge that the clockwork model of the world is defective are not immune to the allure of 'clever' software, because you are spared the task of finding and retaining clever people. Instead you can employ relatively unskilled or inexperienced people – like graduate recruits – to tend the machine.

Problem solved.

Except it isn't. You don't have to take my word for it.

REL, a consultancy that specialises in working capital reduction, estimate that across the top 1000 US companies **$423 billion** is tied up in excess inventory (that's over $400 million per company on average). The number for European companies is E350 billion. And it's not got better over the decade that REL have been running the numbers…if anything, the recent trend is deteriorating.

A whole host of 'reasons' are given for this. 'Financing is historically cheap, so there is no economic incentive to reduce working capital', for instance. But if that's true how come (according to Gartner) companies worldwide are spending $8.3 billion a year on supply chain software? This doesn't square with the story that they are making a rational choice not to make improvements.

My hunch is different.

Producing forecasts and using them to drive supply chain efficiencies is hard work and requires skill. And for many people sophisticated software promises to make the problem go away…and no-one selling this software is going to tell you any different.

I am not anti-software at all – after all I own a software company! It's just that to me, many companies who invest heavily in 'clever' software are doing the equivalent of buying a car without being able to drive, not knowing where they are heading and why, what terrain they will face or how to plot their position and navigate a course. If you are in this position, buying a car with a 'better' engine is not going to get you closer to your goal.

But most smaller businesses face the challenge of forecasting without sophisticated software. Indeed, the most widely used forecasting model in every type of company sits between your ears. It is called judgment. And because we all use this model every moment of the day to make forecasts there is a tendency for them to think that forecasting is easy – little more than common sense.

But the idea that forecasting is just 'common sense' is just as just as dangerous as 'maths will solve everything'.

FORMAT

Because this book is aimed at a broad audience I have tried to make what can be a complex and dry subject accessible and easily digestible. The content is arranged as a series of bite sized 'lessons' supported by simple graphics to illustrate and reinforce the point being made.

There are two types of lessons.

There are positive lessons: concepts and ideas that you can rely on picked out in blue type like this.

But the territory of forecasting is host to a rich population of myths and misinformation. So, there are also 'negative' lessons about what not to do, and these are shown in a red type.

I have given these 'don't do' lessons equal billing…after all it is usually quicker and easier to stop doing stupid stuff than it is to learn how to do clever stuff.

Also, there is no getting away from the fact that forecasting in business is largely a mathematical exercise I have tried to avoid using formulae in the book. Many readers of this book will not be forecasting practitioners and so will not need to understand the mathematics but even forecasters would do a better job if they better understood the problem they were trying to solve before hitting the keyboard. In places, to make the topic accessible I have deliberately oversimplified complex ideas in a way that will make academic forecasters cringe. These are indicated as follows:

For those who need to explore these topics more deeply there are many excellent technical books on forecasting, some of which I have listed in the appendix, along with some of the more basic formulae you might need.

Elsewhere, where I feel a level of technical detail may be necessary for some readers, I have issued a 'nerd alert', which means unless you are one you can skip this bit for the time being.

Finally, in the interest of simplicity I have based the content on the scenario of a 'sell from stock' business. I recognize that service businesses also create operational forecasts, but the same principles apply so learnings based on a stock scenario can almost always be simply applied.

STRUCTURE

I have structured the book around five key themes.

Most of the books written on forecasting in business focus on forecasting techniques. For the reasons I have explained I will do not more than give an overview of the various approaches to producing forecasts – forecasting models – leaving the technicalities to people better qualified than I am. I have tried to be agnostic on the issue of technique. My favourite approach is simply the one that works best. My aim it to give the reader enough background to make informed decisions about the best approach to use – simple or sophisticated, judgement or statistical.

Technique is clearly central to the forecasting challenge, so forecasting methods comprises one of the five themes.

FORECASTING
METHODS

Simple   Sophisticated

BASIC

However, I think the obsessive focus on this to the exception of everything else has been unhealthy for the practice of forecasting. The other four themes will, I hope, help redress this balance.

First – and most important for anyone with a stake in operational forecasting – there is the question of purpose.

Forecasting is not an end in itself, its purpose is to help businesses make better decisions. Only by understanding this purpose can we make the right choices. And we can only judge whether we have succeeded or not by how well it has fulfilled this purpose. In businesses that sell physical products operational forecasts are used to make replenishment decisions and to help determine how much stock to hold. In service businesses, there are close analogues to orders and stock (e.g. the number of staff needed to service forecast demand).

Success is therefore providing supply planners with the information they need to give customers the desired level of service with the lowest possible level of inventory. This, as we will discover, is not necessarily the same thing as 'high forecast accuracy.'

Next there is the question of understanding the behaviour of the variable you are forecasting. The forecasting of items with stable demand needs to be tackled in a different way to those that have a complex or volatile demand pattern, for instance. You need to make sure that you are properly equipped to cope with the forecasting 'weather conditions'.

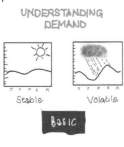

These first three themes provide a basic grounding for anyone associated with forecasting.

The final two are aimed at practitioners wanting to improve their performance, and so are inevitably slightly more technical.

Measuring and interpreting forecast error – i.e. understanding forecast performance – is the fourth theme. Effective measurement is necessary to be able to identify the best forecasting method and understanding where and why performance falls short of the practical optimum is a prerequisite for improving performance. Critically, how forecast performance is measured must relate to the practical purpose it serves in the business.

Finally, like any process, there is always scope for improving forecasts… unnecessary forecast error is waste that should be eliminated wherever possible. This final theme tackles some of the challenges facing any forecaster in the field and provides guidance on how to deal with them.

TERMINOLOGY

I have tried to avoid jargon wherever possible, but some 'buzzwords' are a helpful 'shorthand' that prevent the language getting too convoluted.

The 'specialized' terms that you will come across most frequently are:

Variable: The thing being forecast. Usually assumed to be sales.
Bucket: A unit of time used to measure of actual or forecast values, e.g. a week or month
Demand Series: A sequence of actual sales values.[1]

See the appendix for a list of more technical terms.

---

1 Strictly speaking sales may not be the same as demand – if, for example, there is not sufficient capacity, or if you run out of stock. In the interest of brevity the issue of "constrained demand" is not addressed in this book, but forecast practitioners should always bear it in mind.

DISCLAIMER

In writing this book I am sharing what I have learned, sometimes painfully, in my journey from naïve ignorance to a place where I can claim to be knowledgeable about forecasting in general and an expert on the subject of measuring forecasting performance.

The content of this book is based on academic findings, generally accepted 'good practice' and my own research, but some of it is my opinion based on my personal experience observing and talking to forecasters in the field. To the extent that I cannot 'prove' some of my assertions I beg the forgiveness of my friends in the academic community who have to operate to higher evidential standards.

Most of what I describe is what the best forecasting practitioners already know and do – even if they don't always realise it…with perhaps one important exception.

Few books on forecasting address the most fundamental question: what is the purpose of forecasting? This is important because if we don't know what we are trying to achieve we can't know whether we have succeeded.

For me the answer is clear: to help make better decisions. That sounds simple and straightforward, but it begs more questions: 'what decisions?' And better than what?
Again, the answer seems to me to be obvious:

- Operational forecasts are created in order to help business make decisions about what to order from manufacturers or suppliers and what they need to hold in stock[2].

- Good forecasts have better business outcomes than simply using actual demand to decide what to order and what to hold in reserve.

- A better business outcome is the total benefit of having lower stocks and better customer service by forecasting, less the additional cost of running the process. This is how forecasting adds value.

Consequently, the picture of operational forecasting painted in this book – particularly the final two sections on measurement and management – is viewed through this lens, because the tried and trusted ways of doing these things often don't work very well and so cannot be trusted. To duck this issue by adopting a more conventional stance would be short changing the reader.

My excuse for the absence of academic validation in some places is that given the state of ignorance about the craft of forecasting – even amongst people who have the word in their job title – it is better to have some guidance than none at all. I also think that my background in business gives me a valuable perspective on the practice of forecasting that isn't available from any other source.

I'm striving to provide something that people find useful, not an authoritative textbook, and I am happy to be judged on that basis.

Also, you won't find academic references. This is a book for practitioners not academics. There is a list of recommended books (that do have academic references) at the end if readers would like to learn more.

2 Throughout this book I refer to 'product' and 'inventory' or 'stock' but the concepts and approaches I describe can be applied in exactly the same way to operational forecasting in any domain, such as a service operation, for example. Whether you deal in goods or services you need to estimate what you think the demand is likely to be and how much you need to hold in reserve to deal with the inevitability of your forecast being wrong.

SECTION 1
THE PURPOSE OF FORECASTING

Target service level   At lowest cost

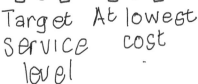

Basic

Forecasting is not an end in itself - it is the means to an end.

Success in forecasting, like any other endeavour, can only be determined by how well the process fulfills its purpose.

The purpose of forecasting is explained in this section.

What IS a forecast?

First of all, we need to be absolutely clear what a forecast is – and what it isn't.

A forecast is a best estimate of future outcomes. An expectation of what you think WILL happen.

This is different to a target, which is what you would LIKE to happen. An aspiration.

Ideally, you would like to bring your expectations in line with your aspirations, but more often than not there will be a gap between them. Gaps are important because they tell you that you need to do something different.

Problems start when people get mixed up between forecasts and targets. Very often this happens without anybody ever realizing it.

For example, when people feel good about 'beating their forecast' they are using the forecast as a target… and as a result the forecast will stop doing the job it needs to do. It will become a bad forecast.

If this is what you are doing, stop it!

TAKEOUT

Don't get forecasts confused with targets. A forecast is an expectation - a best guess of what is really going to happen. A target is an aspiration - what we would like to happen.

A target is an ASPIRATION

TARGET

a sign we need to do something different

Gap

FORECAST

A forecast is an EXPECTATION

Forecasts are not the same as budgets or plans

You can't have a conversation with someone about anything unless you have a common language, and conversations about forecasting suffer from the inconsistent and undisciplined way certain key terms are used.

Forecasts describe expectations about the future, and these are likely to be different to **budgets**, as these are often the source of targets – an aspiration for the future.

Forecasts and budgets are not the same as, but are based on, **plans,** which are sets of intended actions (and their anticipated impact) and **assumptions** about the future. Those underpinning forecasts will differ from those that informed the budget as new information becomes available and plans are changed in response.

Forecasts, budgets, plans and assumptions are closely related, but they do not describe the same thing.

> TAKEOUT
>
> Don't confuse forecasts with budgets, plans or assumptions. Forecasts describe expectations but budgets are a source of aspirations. A plan is a set of intended actions that - along with data about the past and assumptions about the future - are used to create forecasts.

The different roles of forecasts, plans and budgets

BUDGET
(TARGET)

Gap

FORECAST

Gap

Gap to budget (target) drives changes to plans

FORECAST PROCESS

ACTUAL THEN

ACTUAL NOW

PLANS
a.
b.
c.
intended actions

FORECAST METHOD

ACTUAL PERFORMANCE

ASSUMED FUTURE CONDITIONS

AND ACTUAL CONDITIONS

Gap to actual used to improve forecast process

Different kinds of forecasts

This book is focused on operational forecasting – the stuff you do to determine what you need to buy, produce, hold in stock or otherwise give your customers what they need.

This differs from other kinds of forecasting that you might do in your business.

Long term forecasting may be needed to help an organization make strategic choices about where and what to invest in. This kind of forecasts help organizations to ADAPT.

Medium-term business forecasts help STEER the business by managing the allocation of resources in order to deliver business performance.

Operational forecasts help businesses RESPOND to demand in the short term, and because the purpose of operational forecasting differs from medium and long terms forecasting, the process tends to be different as well.

In particular, operational forecasts are done in greater detail. Since your customers want to buy a particular kind of say, shoe, in a particular size and colour, producing a forecast for shoes in general won't help you provide good customer service.

Also, most businesses (at least the ones that survive) respond to demand reasonably quickly, so operational forecasts need to be refreshed very frequently.

In summary, operational forecasts are short term, very detailed and frequently refreshed and used to help businesses respond effectively and efficiently to customer demand. Because operational forecasting is a high volume, variety and velocity process it tends to be more reliant on automated mathematical processes than other kinds of forecasts.

TAKEOUT

Don't get operational forecasts confused with other kinds of forecasts which have different purposes and processes. Operational forecasts are short term, detailed and used to help businesses respond to changes in demand.

LONG TERM STRATEGIC FORECASTS

are used to make **CHOICES**

MEDIUM TERM BUSINESS FORECASTS

are used to **STEER** the business

SHORT TERM OPERATIONAL FORECASTS

are used to **RESPOND** to events

All operational forecasting is based on the same principles

There are many different kinds of operational forecasts – forecasts of sales of products, of demand for services, for power…the list is endless. And there are many different ways that operational forecasts can be generated.

But all operational forecasts serve the same purposes, irrespective of the domain. They are required to determine:

First, how much 'X' is needed in the system to meet anticipated demand within a lead time that is acceptable to the customer. Second, how much spare 'X' is needed to provide a defined level of customer service given the inherent uncertainty in any forecast.

'X' could be products, people or power, for example. And 'spare X' could be safety stock, people on call or power plants ready to be fired up on demand. But whatever the 'X', the basic principles underpinning the forecast process, and how it is used to help make decisions, are the same.

The examples in this book is based on a business selling from stock but the lessons can be directly applied to all other kinds of operational forecasting.

TAKEOUT

Any kind of operational forecasting serves the same purpose: what needs to be supplied to meet demand and what needs to be kept in reserve to ensure that unforecast demand can be met, consistent with desired service levels. Learnings are transferable between domains.

The principles of Operational Forecasting are the same

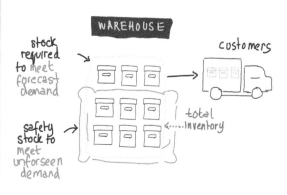

WAREHOUSE

customers

stock required to meet forecast demand

safety stock to meet unforseen demand

total inventory

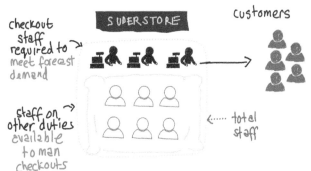

SUPERSTORE

customers

checkout staff required to meet forecast demand

staff on other duties available to man checkouts if required

total staff

Why operational forecasting is important

In an ideal world, we wouldn't need forecasts. Things would happen and businesses would simply respond to them.

In the real world, this often just isn't possible.

If you have invested millions in a factory to make Product X, you can't instantly switch to making Product Y.

And even if it were physically possible to respond, it might not be economically sensible to do so. It doesn't make sense to manufacture say, a single loaf of bread, every time a customer asks for one.

Instead, many – perhaps most – manufacturers and retailers build stock in anticipation of future need – and this requires a forecast.

The forecast could be very simple like: 'I forecast I will sell the same number of units in this coming period as I did in the last' or it could be very sophisticated, based on complex statistical algorithms.

Whatever the method used to produce a forecast it is important to get it as right as you can.

Having too much stock is very costly. Cash is tied up in unproductive assets, and it costs money to store and transport it to where it is required.

But not having enough inventory means that customer service will suffer and sales may be lost.

> ### TAKEOUT
> Pay special attention to operational forecasting since it is one of the few business processes which impacts cash, costs AND customer service.

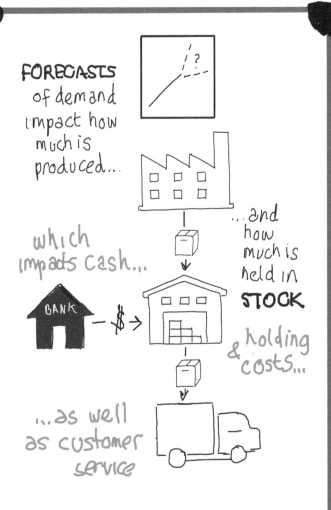

FORECASTS of demand impact how much is produced...

...and how much is held in **STOCK**

which impacts cash...

& holding costs...

...as well as customer service

The quality of forecasts matters...a lot

It is difficult to precisely estimate the business impact of forecast quality partly because it impacts so many variables in ways that are not easy to isolate:

- Inventory levels
- Financing costs
- Warehousing costs
- Transport costs
- Expediting costs (incurred when extra product is required at short notice to meet unforecast demand)
- Lost sales

In addition, poor forecasting can impact the service performance of an organisation, which can have a long-term reputational impact that is difficult to quantify.

Also – as we will discover – it is not straightforward to measure the quality of forecasting in a meaningful way. As a result, most businesses have no idea whether their forecasts are good, bad or indifferent.

What is for sure is that poor forecasting is wasteful and the business impact is huge.

I estimate the unnecessary operating costs of poor forecasting account for 2% of the cost of sales – perhaps 10m for each billion of revenue (assuming a margin of 50%) – and that's not counting the benefits associated with better customer service.

But the 'low hanging fruit' comes from reduced inventory, that across the top 1000 US companies is estimated to be worth $423 billion, with the best performers operating with less than half the level of stock than the median (14 days inventory cover compared to 35).

TAKEOUT

Focus on operational forecasting to improve the bottom line. Poor quality forecasting is the largest unrecognised source of waste in many businesses.

Forecasting is a (very) good investment

Improving the forecasting process is probably one of the most attractive investment propositions that a business can have.

One of the ways in which finance people look at investment is to measurement the 'pay back' – the length of time it takes for a initial investment to be recovered by savings.

When I was a financial analyst I normally regarded a three year pay back as acceptable, but an investment in forecasting that helps reduce stocks can pay back in three months or even sooner. I can't think of any other kind of investment that is this attractive from a financial point of view.

The reason for this stellar performance is that when an improvement in forecasting results in a reduction in stock the cash benefit is immediate. Because the investment pays back so quickly the cost savings from a reduction in warehousing, obsolescence and so on over the longer term are almost like free money. And that's before you factor in the intangible benefits of better customer service.

This sounds great. What's the catch?

The catch is that in order to make this work you need to do three things:
1.   Make a measurable improvement in forecast quality
2.   Ensure that it is translated into reduced inventory
3.   Sustain the improvement. If you take your foot off the gas you can easily go backwards.

In other words, you need to work at it, which requires management to understand and commit to the forecast process.

TAKEOUT

Don't just throw money at forecasting. Back up investments with knowledge and sustained hard work and you will be generously rewarded.

Investments in forecasting improvement pays back very quickly

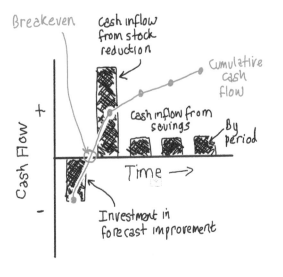

Breakeven

cash inflow from stock reduction

Cumulative cash flow

Cash inflow from savings

By period

Cash Flow

+

−

Time →

Investment in forecast improvement

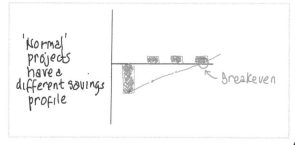

'Normal' projects have a different savings profile

Breakeven

Forecasting is not compulsory

Operational forecasting is important but it is not mandatory.

Operational forecasts are used to make sure that a business can respond effectively to customer demand for its products or services.

But, if you could respond instantly to customer demand then you wouldn't need to forecast at all.

Since most businesses cannot respond quickly enough, they have to produce or buy products in advance of demand and hold reserves in the form of safety stock or spare resources to be sure of satisfying customer demand. The level of buffer needed is determined by how well you can anticipate demand – how good your forecast is.

The very simplest approach is to assume 'no change' – that you will sell the same tomorrow as you sold today. This is sometimes called 'Kanban' after the approach to replenishment used in 'Lean' manufacturing. Forecasters call this the 'naïve forecast'.

Professional forecasters might not regard this a 'real' forecast because it is very crude. But anything more sophisticated is only worthwhile if it is capable of outperforming this simple 'one out, one in' method of replenishment. If it <u>can</u> do a better job of anticipating demand, less stock will be required to provide a given level of customer service, which is the only reason why more sophisticated forecasts are needed.

TAKEOUT

Always remember: the goal of operational forecasting is not to produce accurate forecasts; it is to make better replenishment decisions than by <u>not</u> forecasting.

Forecasting can only be justified if it can
beat simple replenishment

'SIMPLE' REPLENISHMENT

'one in - one out'
or
'kanban'

(large) buffer stock
to cover variation
in demand

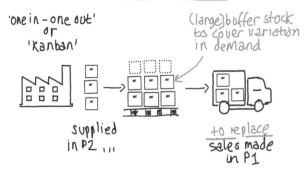

supplied
in P2 ...

to replace
sales made
in P1

FORECAST DRIVEN REPLENISHMENT

(smaller?) buffer
stock to cover
variation in
forecast error

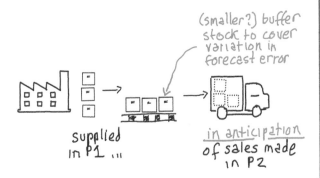

supplied
in P1 ...

in anticipation
of sales made
in P2

SECTION 2
UNDERSTANDING DEMAND

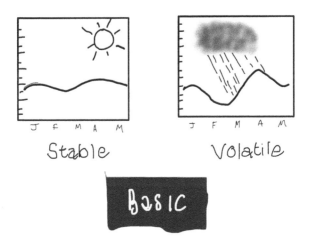

Stable   Volatile

Basic

Success in forecasting is based on a good understanding of the characteristics of the variables that you are attempting to predict.

Operational demand data has peculiar characteristics that are important for forecasters, or those responsible for managing them, to understand.

This section describes those demand patterns that are of most significance for the process of forecasting.

Data Series are different – and it matters to forecasters

The nature of demand that is to be forecast, as represented by patterns in the historic data series, is the most important consideration for the forecasting practitioner.

Because operational forecasts are used to help businesses respond to demand, they have to be made at the level of demand, i.e. by individual end product (typically SKU) and stock holding location.

The data series concerned may be continuous – i.e. with a value in every period - and be relatively easy to forecast, particularly if there is not too much change from one period to the next. But at the detailed level at which forecasts are made simple patterns like this may be uncommon.

Sometimes a data series is continuous but has periods with exceptionally high values, and so looks very 'lumpy'. As it is often difficult to forecast when these spikes will occur and how big they will be, forecasters can often do no better than estimate a range of potential values for these spikes.

At the extreme, intermittent data series have a large number of periods with zero values. These are even more difficult to forecast as there is often no way of knowing whether any particular period will have a zero value or not. So, the best that a forecaster can do is to estimate a good average.

TAKE OUT

Make sure that you understand the characteristics of the data series that you are attempting to forecast. They can be continuous or intermittent; smooth or lumpy.

TYPES OF DEMAND PATTERN

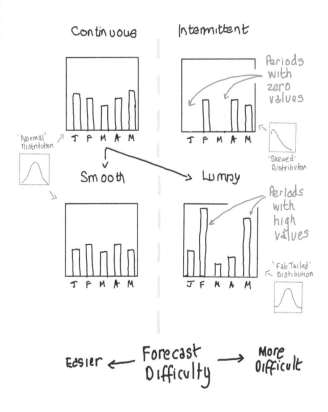

Continuous

Intermittent

Periods with zero values

'Normal' Distribution

J F M A M

J F M A M

'Skewed' Distribution

Smooth → Lumpy

Periods with high values

J F M A M

J F M A M

'Fat Tailed' Distribution

Easier ← Forecast Difficulty → More Difficult

Forecasting is not easy

All forecasting is based on one very major assumption: that the future is like the past.

OK - the future has got to be somewhat like the past, because if it weren't we would not be alive to witness it. If there weren't a lot of predictability then everything we did would be a massive gamble – a throw of the dice with no idea what the outcome would be.

But it is never EXACTLY like the past because the world never stays still. Every moment of every day is, in its own way, unique. So, if you made the same decisions day after day it is unlikely that the outcome would be the same because the world around you will have changed. And, of course, businesses employ a lot of people whose job is to make things different, as do all of their customers and competitors.

So don't think that you can predict the future…exactly.

In particular, it is very difficult to predict discontinuities – breaks in the established pattern of behaviour of a variable. For example, when you add or lose a customer, or a competitor launches a new product.

On a smaller scale, there are may be 'spikes' – temporary changes in behaviour patterns – that are also tricky to forecast. This might be the result of a promotion, or perhaps an issue in the distribution system.

Things like breaks and spikes are difficult to forecast, so often the best thing that you can do is to adapt. Identify changes as quickly as possible and change your future forecast to reflect the new reality.

TAKEOUT

Don't expect forecasts to be accurate predictions. All forecast techniques assume that the future is going to be somewhat like the past so they are incapable of anticipating changes in patterns of demand. Instead, build the capability to spot and respond quickly.

Forecasting is possible because
the future is usually like the past

Past ← — Now — → Future

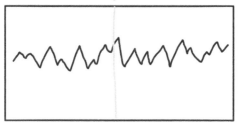

But sometimes it isn't

Discontinuities   Spikes

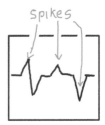

Which makes forecasting challenging

It is not possible to predict the future

There is another reason why the future cannot be predicted – noise.

What is noise?

The job of a forecasters is to detect the signal in past data and to project it into the future. A signal represents the 'true' state of a system and so is potentially forecastable. Noise is everything that is not a signal. And because noise is random it is not forecastable in principle.

Let's illustrate the idea with an example.

Start up the stopwatch feature on your smartphone and stop it after a few seconds. Say you stopped it after 2.54 seconds.

Now zero the display and this time try to stop your watch at EXACTLY the same time – 2.54 seconds. Go ahead and try it a few times.

2.54 is the signal in this system, but even though you have full knowledge of it, I guarantee that you will fail to stop the watch at this value.

The difference between any two numbers in this data series is noise. It is possible that you might have some idea why you failed – perhaps you were distracted - but more likely you will have no idea why.

This simple game illustrates that noise is an unavoidable fact of life and why it is unforecastable.

In the context of forecasting this means that even if you had perfect knowledge of the behaviour of a system - an unlikely scenario – your forecast would still be 'wrong' to some degree.

Forecasts can only ever be right 'on average'.

TAKEOUT

Don't expect perfect forecasts because data is always infected by random noise, which is unforecastable in principle. Forecasts can only ever be right 'on average'.

Data is made up of two things:

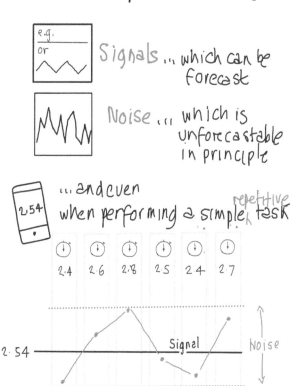

e.g.

or

Signals ... which can be forecast

Noise ... which is unforecastable in principle

2.54

... and even when performing a simple~~,~~ repetitive task

2.4   2.6   2.8   2.5   2.4   2.7

2·54 ——————————— Signal —————— Noise

It is <u>impossible</u> to avoid noise

It is not easy to spot noise

One of the problems that forecasters have with noise is that it often doesn't look like noise to us.

Noise gets its name from radio engineers who were the first people who had to find practical ways of managing it. But they had a relatively easy job because when you have lots of data points and a known signal (such as a piece of music) it's easier to spot noise.

But if you do not know what your signal 'looks like' in advance and you have much less data - perhaps only get one new data point a month - it is much harder to work out what is noise and what is the signal that you need to base your forecasts on.

Don't expect a noisy data series to neatly zig-zag from one period to the next. A repetitive pattern like this is not the randomness that you would expect from noise.

The fact is, that when it comes to noise you cannot trust your intuition since our brains are hardwired to look for patterns, and we will see them where there don't exist.

It's easy to test this.

Just look at some clouds and you are almost guaranteed to 'see' recognizable shapes in them. We know that these shapes aren't there but it is difficult to 'unsee' them once we have spotted them.

It is just the same with the data that we use to inform our forecasts. We cannot trust our intuitions to spot noise so we have to use statistical methods instead.

> ### TAKEOUT
> Don't think that you can spot noise, even though it is always present.
> It can only be inferred by using statistical logic.

Our brains are 'hard wired' for patterns ...

noise

noise (not a rabbit)

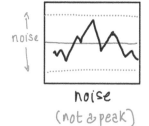

noise
(not a peak)

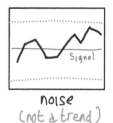

noise
(not a trend)

from statistics

... so we need help to 'see' noise

(particularly when we don't have much data)

Types of Signal

Forecasts are estimates of the future value of a variable, often based on an understanding of the behaviour of a signal in the past.

There are three basic archetypes:

1. First, it could be flat – a stationary signal.

2. Secondly it could be a trend. This trend could be up or down. It could look like a straight line (linear growth or decline) or it could be a curve (exponential or non-linear). Trends are the dominant feature of new or declining lines of business.

3. Thirdly it could display a repetitive pattern of behaviour. In forecasting jargon this is known as 'seasonality', but the cycles needn't have anything to do with the weather. For example, we often see seasonality in daily data because people behave differently during the week and at the weekend. You need a long data series to be sure that changes in demand are truly seasonal.

Any single data series will most likely have a mix of these patterns – which may be more or less pronounced - overlaid by a greater or lesser extent of noise. And the patterns can change at any time or be disrupted by events that temporarily disturb established patterns.

Because forecasting methods need to be tailored to the type of signal and the level of noise, an understanding of the behaviour of signals is the foundation of the craft of forecasting.

TAKEOUT

Understand the behaviour of a data series before trying to forecast it.

Three
different types of **signal**

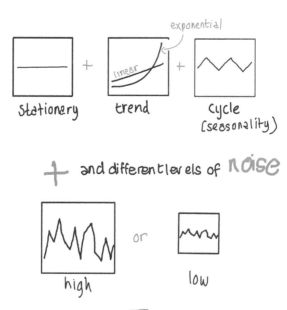

Stationary   trend   Cycle
                              (seasonality)

╋ and different levels of **noise**

high   or   low

═

(and possibly changing/disrupted)
all mixed up together, make a **data series**

The buckets used to measure
demand changes the characteristics of the data

The characteristics of a data series are influenced by the way it is measured.

More aggregated data is inherently less noisy than low-level data because noise cancels itself out in the process of aggregation.

For example, data that is smooth and continuous when it is measured in monthly buckets may become lumpy when it is managed in weekly buckets and intermittent in daily buckets, which makes forecasting more challenging.

But while forecasting at a high level might be easier, it can degrade forecast quality because patterns in low level data may be lost.

For example, there is often a very pronounced cyclical pattern in daily data because demand data usually varies with the days of the week, which is lost when it is grouped into weekly buckets. Conversely, cyclical patterns due to weather or holiday effects might be masked by noise in daily data but may be easy to detect in monthly data.

In practice, the level at which data is captured is also influenced by the way in which forecasts are used. For example, if stock needs to be replenished daily, you will need daily data and daily forecasts.

TAKEOUT
When determining the level at which to capture data balance the ease of forecasting with the use to which the forecasts are put.

The buckets used to capture data affects the patterns we can see

BIG BUCKETS = LOW NOISE

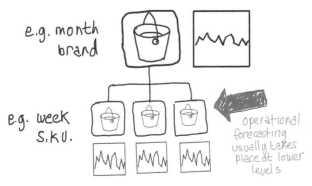

e.g. month
brand

e.g. week
S.K.U.

operational
forecasting
usually takes
place at lower
levels

SMALL BUCKETS = HIGH NOISE

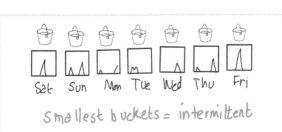

Sat Sun Mon Tue Wed Thu Fri

Smallest buckets = intermittent

Characteristics of operational demand data

The characteristics of operational demand data define the challenge faced by forecasters.

Typically, it is:
- Detailed, and because of this it is
- Infected with high levels of noise, with
- Complex patterns of signals

Because of the large numbers of product lines, the frequency at which they need to be forecast and the complexity inherent in the data, operational forecasting tends to make greater use of mathematical techniques based on an analysis of historic data than other forms of forecasting, which rely more on judgement.

This makes it easier to automate the forecast process, but it does not reduce the need for expertise or knowledge of the business

Sophisticated software needs skilled users. Also, low level operational demand data is also easily perturbed by non-recurring events, many of which are consciously engineered (like price changes and promotions), and patterns of signals may change permanently.

Because the past is not always a reliable guide to the future, well targeted judgemental intervention in the forecast process is required. Also, wherever there is a new line of business, or an old one is retired, methods based on historical analysis are less useful. Both of these require understanding of the business as well as forecasting skill.

> TAKEOUT
>
> Automate operational forecasting but beware when attempting to de-skill or outsource the process.

Reasons why automated methods are suited to operational forecasting

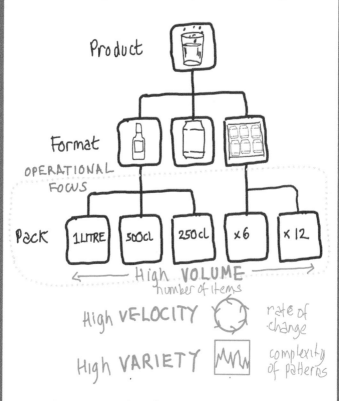

Product

Format

OPERATIONAL FOCUS

Pack | 1 LITRE | 500cL | 250cL | x6 | x12

←— High VOLUME —→
number of items

High VELOCITY ↻ rate of change

High VARIETY ⩗ complexity of patterns

...with targeted judgemental interventions

33

SECTION 3
FORECASTING METHODS

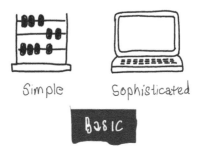

Simple   Sophisticated

Basic

There is an enormous range of methods available to forecasters, many
of which are too complex for non mathematicians to understand. But
some grasp of how these models work is essential for everyone involved
in the process. Otherwise it is not possible to make sound decisions
about what method to use.

But you don't need to become an expert.

Managing a forecast process is like driving a car. You don't need to be an
engineer to drive one but you do need to know when you need one and to
be able to distinguish good from bad advice.

Every method has strengths but also weaknesses and sometimes too
much knowledge and personal investment in learning the subtleties of a
particular technique can lead to practitioners falling in love with it, and
in the process losing sight of the ultimate goal - improving performance
using whatever method works best.

This section provides an overview of the most common forecasting
techniques.

The forecasting challenge

It is not possible to forecast future outcome precisely.

Only the signal is potentially forecastable – noise is unforecastable in principle.

And all forecasts assume that the future is more or less like the past. But all past data is infected by noise, which hides the signal.

And signals can and do change.

The challenge is to spot the patterns of signals hidden in data about the past, to project these into the future and to forecast whether, when and how these patterns will change.

And it is not possible to know in advance whether any particular forecasting technique will work. Sophistication is no guarantee of performance.

The only way is to measure how successful a forecast process has actually been at estimating the signal.

TAKEOUT

In forecasting, there are no marks for style, only results matter.

The forecasting challenge

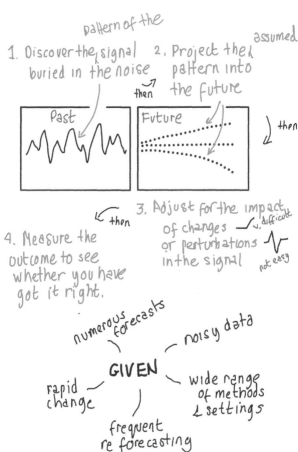

1. Discover the <u>pattern of the</u> signal buried in the noise

2. Project the <u>assumed</u> pattern into the future

then →

Past

Future

↧ then

3. Adjust for the impact of changes or perturbations in the signal   v. difficult / not easy

← then

4. Measure the outcome to see whether you have got it right.

numerous forecasts

noisy data

GIVEN

rapid change

wide range of methods & settings

frequent re forecasting

Three ways to produce forecasts

There are three ways to produce a forecast, each of which are based on some kind of model – a simplified representation of reality.

The most common mathematical model used in operational forecasting involves extrapolation from the past using statistical methods.

These are sometimes referred to as univariate methods (because they only use one variable), or extrapolative or time series models.

A second set of methods use causal models. An example of a causal model is when you use forecast temperatures and knowledge of public holidays to predict ice cream sales.

These are sometimes called multivariate methods, because they forecast one variable (sales) using more than one variable.

Apart from the use of mathematics, these two methods have one other thing in common – they both assume that the future will be like the past. Causal models assume that while the value of the variables driving the model may change, the relationship between variables does not. Extrapolation models reflect changes in a single variable, but relatively slowly.

But the most common method used in forecasting involves judgement, where the model in use sits in someone's head. Forecasts can be 100% judgemental or judgement might be applied in the form of an adjustment to a mathematically derived model.

Judgemental models are the only way that new knowledge – such as market intelligence - can be incorporated into forecasts. Only people can 'know' that a customer is going to stop buying from you, or estimate the sales of a completely new product…an algorithm cannot because it is a prisoner of history.

In practice, often all three methods are used, sometimes in combination.

TAKEOUT

Make sure that you use the right sort of model to generate forecasts: time series, casual or judgemental methods, or a combination of the three. Mathematical models are based on the analysis of history. Only judgement can anticipate change.

Three Types of forecasting model

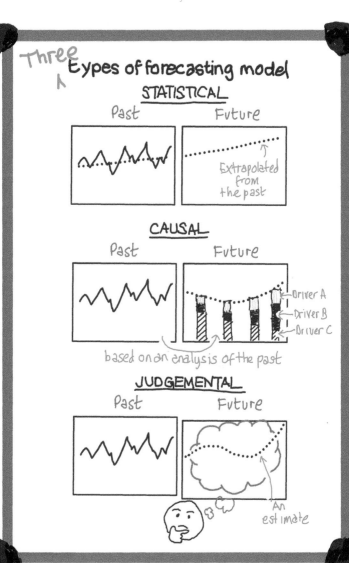

STATISTICAL

Past   Future

Extrapolated
from
the past

CAUSAL

Past   Future

Driver A
Driver B
Driver C

based on an analysis of the past

JUDGEMENTAL

Past   Future

An
estimate

39

Forecasting by extrapolating from historic time series

Extrapolative – or time series - models are the most common mathematical models used in forecasting because they are relatively simple and often work as well as, if not better, than more sophisticated approaches.

Time series models typically use a particular type of moving average to generate a forecast. Exponential smoothing gives more weight to more recent data points and like all averaging methods it is based on the assumption that the trend represents the signal and any variation around it is noise.

Extrapolation doesn't require any understanding of what is driving the behaviour of the data series. It is purely data driven, so every time a model is run (usually every period) it responds to the new data by generating a new forecast.

The most basic time series model simply forecasts the <u>level</u> of a variable. This is called single exponential smoothing.

More sophisticated time series models forecast trends (e.g. double exponential smoothing) and seasonality – repetitive patterns of behaviour whatever the cause (e.g. triple exponential smoothing). The specific methods are usually referred to by the name of their creator: e.g. Brown's, Holt or Holt-Winter's methods.

All these models are types of ARIMA models, which can be made sensitive to other characteristics of a data series such as 'momentum' ('auto correlation' – e.g. a Box Jenkins model).

Whatever model is chosen it will also need to be tuned by adjusting the weighting used in the averaging process, and more sophisticated models generally have more parameters that need tuning and more history for them on which to base their calculations. This makes these models more sensitive, which can be a good thing. But they can also be more likely to mistake noise for signals, so they may perform no better than simpler, cruder models.

TAKEOUT

Use time series models where it is safe to assume that trends will continue in the future. Such methods are simple and reliable and have become the workhorse of mathematical forecasting.

Three types of statistical models

SINGLE EXPONENTIAL SMOOTHING (S.E.S)

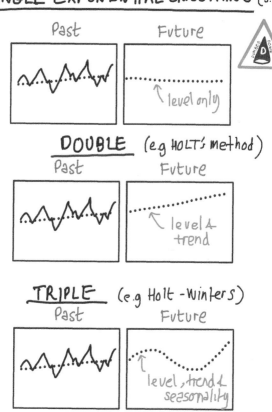

Past | Future

↖ level only

DOUBLE (e.g HOLT's method)

Past | Future

↖ level & trend

TRIPLE (e.g Holt-Winters)

Past | Future

↑ level, trend & seasonality

Forecasting using causal models

Causal models assume that you know – or can discover – the factors driving the behaviour of a variable.

They do so by mathematically modeling the relationship between the thing you are trying to forecast (the dependent variable) and the drivers of its behaviour (the independent variables).

Used in the right way and in the right circumstances, these techniques can be extremely powerful, particularly as dummy variables can be introduced so that the impact of intermittent events such as public holidays or sales promotions can be modelled separately from 'business as usual'.

The downsides of this approach are:
1. Care needs to be exercised to avoid confusing correlation with causation. For example, the sales of men's shorts are correlated with those of ice cream but one does not cause the other. Both are caused by another variable – the weather.
2. It depends on being able to forecast the independent variable well. For example, if weather is a key driver but it can't be accurately forecast more than 7 days out a driver based model using monthly buckets will not be accurate.
3. Building causal models requires skill and time and usually a lot of historic data.
4. It assumes that relationships between independent and dependent variables will persist e.g. that shorts will continue to be worn only in hot weather
5. Like all sophisticated models, it is prone to mistake noise for signals and so may not outperform cruder methods.

TAKEOUT

Use causal models where you have a good understanding of the drivers of demand, how they interact with each other and you are able to forecast them well.

How causal modelling works

Past

DECOMPOSE

causal
factors
(drivers)

e.g weather

e.g relative
price

e.g market

FORECAST

RECOMBINE

Future

43

Forecasting using judgement

Despite the advances made in forecasting technology in the last few decades, judgement is still the most common method used in forecasting.

Judgement can be used on its own, for example when a sales team is asked to forecast demand. Or it can be used in combination with other methods, such as when judgement is used to add market intelligence or domain knowledge (such as customer intentions) to statistically generated baseline forecasts.

But judgement is fickle and can easily be biased by wishful thinking, perverse motivations or simple errors of logic. And, as we have seen, our brains are notoriously bad at separating signals from noise, displaying a tendency to see patterns in data where none exist. Also, judgement is often applied in a thoughtless way, as when forecasts are overridden because someone doesn't like the answer.

As a result, some of the very best, but also some of the very worst, forecasts are based on judgemental methods.

In addition, generating judgemental forecasts or judgmentally adjusting statistically generated forecasts is a very labour intensive process.

For all these reasons many academics, software vendors and cost-conscious managers would like to engineer judgement out of the forecast process.

But judgement cannot be avoided altogether. Judgement is even involved in building, choosing and tuning any kind of mathematical model.

The choice faced by managers is not whether to use judgement but how to ensure that it is applied appropriately and effectively.

How judgement is used in forecasting

Past

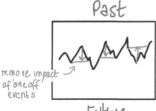

remove impact of one-off events

Adjusting (cleaning) history
used by algorithms to generate forecasts

Future

add in impact of new "events"

Adjusting forecasts
generated by algorithms

Future

Creating forecasts
instead of using algorithms

ARIMA?
S.E.S? Holts?
Causal? Judgement?
Customer?
Product?

Choosing models/ methods/ parameters

Three types of bias in judgemental forecasting

Problems with judgement in forecasting usually manifest themselves as bias. Bias is the tendency to consistently under or over forecast.

There are three types of bias:

1. Cognitive Biases

Our brains are prone to making logical flaws that manifest themselves as biased forecasts. Examples of this include 'confirmation bias', which is the tendency to take more notice of evidence when it confirms our pre-existing views and 'availability bias', where we tend to be unduly influenced by the most recent or eye-catching piece of data. 'Anchoring' is the reluctance to move from a pre-existing position, such as a target or the forecasts from the last period, even in the face of evidence.

2. Social Biases

We have a tendency to modify and moderate our views to conform with those of the group or influential individuals, particularly if our pre-existing views differ to the norm. This can often happen in 'forecast review' meetings, for example.

3. Motivational Biases

Forecasts are frequently distorted by organisational rewards or punishments. For example, when changes to forecasts are praised or criticised, or forecasts are used to set targets.

Processes should be designed to minimise the chances of infection by bias, but continuous measurement is the only cure.

> ### TAKEOUT
> Judgement is likely to be infected by bias. Measurement provides the diagnosis and the cure.

Three Sources of bias in judgemental forecasting

Cognitive

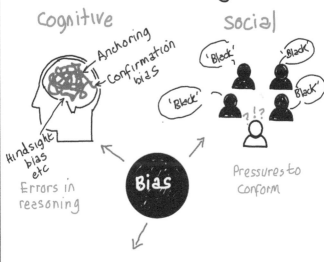

Anchoring
← Confirmation bias
Hindsight bias etc
Errors in reasoning

Social

'Black' 'Black'
'Black' 'Black'
'Black' ?!?

Pressures to conform

Bias

Motivational

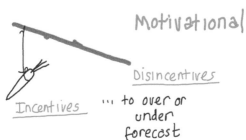

Incentives

Disincentives

... to over or under forecast

The better the fit to history – (sometimes) the worse the forecast method

Mathematical forecasting techniques also have weaknesses, particularly if they are applied in a thoughtless way.

Probably the most common error made by those with some mathematical knowledge, but no forecasting experience, is to confuse how well a model fits to the historical data with its ability to predict the future.

The first step in building a mathematical forecasting model is to choose an algorithm that explains history. It's very tempting to assume that the model that fits best to the history – as measured by something like the R^2 metric – will provide the best forecast.

But that would be wrong.

The reason for this is that when an algorithm fits to history it doesn't know the difference between signal and noise. And the more sensitive/sophisticated the algorithm, the greater the chances that it will fit to noise rather than the signal.

And as we have already discovered, noise – being random - doesn't repeat itself. So, to the extent that the algorithm fits to noise it will be a poor predictor of the future.

This very common problem is called 'overfitting'.

TAKEOUT

Don't confuse model fit with forecast performance. A better fit to the past can sometimes result in a <u>worse</u> fit to the future.

How overfitting destroys forecast quality

This data randomly varies around 0.5

R^2 = 'goodness' of fit (1.0 = perfect)

data

so we know this is the best forecast

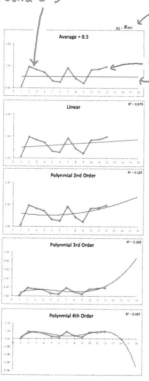

As the <u>models</u> get more SOPHISTICATED the 'fit' IMPROVES but the <u>forecast</u> DETERIORATES

How to avoid overfitting

Overfitting is where a chosen forecasting algorithm fits 'too tightly' to the historical record. Effectively it 'sees' patterns in the data that don't exist because they are manifestations of random noise…the mathematical equivalent of seeing faces in clouds.

There is only one way to ensure that you do not fall into this trap – measure actual forecast performance, not (just) the fit to history.

In practice, this is achieved by using a 'hold out sample' to evaluate the performance of different algorithms.

This is done by dividing the historical data into two sets.

The first part ('in sample' or 'training data') is used to select those algorithms that have a 'good enough' fit to that chunk of the historic record.

The second part ('the hold out sample' or validation data) is used to select and tune the algorithm that best 'predicts' this part of the historic record.

The fact that an algorithm has forecast well in the past is no guarantee that it will work in the future, and also the pattern of signals can change. The only way to ensure that you have the right algorithms is to routinely measure and analyse forecast error.

And it is good practice to periodically repeat the model fitting process – but not too frequently as this could lead to overfitting as well.

TAKEOUT

Select forecasting algorithms based on their ability to forecast a hold out sample. Measure forecast errors to ensure that the predictive ability of the chosen methods has not deteriorated.

How to avoid overfitting

1. Take a data series

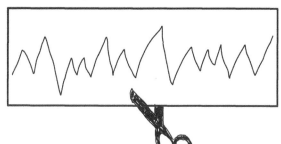

2. chop it into two

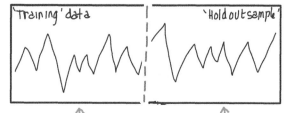

'Training' data   'Hold out sample'

↑
3. Use this part to generate forecasting models

↑
4. Use this to find out which one forecasts best

Sophisticated methods are (often) no better than simple ones

Mathematical forecasting methods have been used in operations since the 1950's when the first time series methods were invented, and since then a steady stream of more sophisticated methods have appeared on the market. Most recently methods that claim to be capable of 'learning', using Bayesian statistical methods or artificial neural networks, have become fashionable.

Software vendors like to claim that such sophisticated methods are superior, which is a message that many managers would like to believe because it promises a way out of the need to employ skilled resources in an unfashionable area of the business.

Unfortunately, simple methods often outperform more sophisticated ones. This has been validated many times, most notably in the 'M' forecasting competitions run by Spyros Makridakis.[3]

The reason is simple.

All mathematical methods are based on extrapolation from the past. And the more sophisticated the method the more likely it is to confuse signals with noise and detect patterns that do not exist.

TAKEOUT

Don't assume that sophistication is a guarantee of good forecasts - it might even make them worse.

3   Spyros Makridakis is a professor of forecasting who first ran a competition to measure the performance of different forecasting methods in 1982 (M1). His initial objective was to prove the value of sophisticated forecasting methods to sceptics in business, but he ended up demonstrating the opposite – that simple methods often outperform complex ones.
This conclusion was, unsurprisingly, unpopular in the academic community. So, he ran two more forecasting competitions in 1993 and 2000 (M2 and M3) with larger data sets and involving more forecasting experts, in response to criticisms of his research methodology. The results, however, supported the original conclusion: simple methods often work best.

Sophistication doesn't guarantee success: results from the 'M3' forecasting competition

.... conducted under 'laboratory' conditions

Best at top   method/software used

Rank	Method	RAE	Type	Sophistication
1	ForecastPro	0.67	Expert	
2	B-J automatic	0.68	ARIMA	
3	Dampen	0.70	Statistical	
4	Comb S-H-D	0.71	Statistical	
5	Holts Winter	0.71	Statistical	
6	Forecast X	0.72	Expert	
7	Holt	0.72	Statistical	
8	Theta	0.73	Decomposition	
9	SES	0.73	Simple	
10	ARAMA	0.74	ARIMA	
11	AAM1	0.74	ARIMA	
12	PP-Autocast	0.76	Statistical	
13	Autobox1	0.76	ARIMA	
14	Autobox3	0.78	ARIMA	
15	Naive 2	0.79	Simple	
16	Autobox2	0.79	ARIMA	
17	Flores-Pearce 1	0.80	Expert	
18	Automat-Ann	0.81	Expert	
19	AAM2	0.82	ARIMA	
20	Robust-Trend	0.86	Statistical	
21	Theta-Sm	0.88	Statistical	
22	RBF	0.88	Expert	
23	Flores-Pearce 2	0.95	Expert	
24	Smartfcs	0.96	Expert	
	Average	**0.78**		

Annotations:
- 'simple' SES performed adequately (6% below best)
- Average level of performance
- many 'sophisticated' Expert systems had below average performance

Expert = software using autoselection algorithms

- no causal methods used
- 300 Leg 1 forecasts
- RAE < 1.0 = value adding

53

The methods used in different software packages are not unique

The majority of forecasting algorithms have been developed independently, by practitioners and academics, and subsequently adopted by software companies.

So, beware of vendors who claim that their methods are 'new and unique'. Where they are proprietary, you should not assume that they are better than 'normal' methods because they have not been subject to independent challenge and the validation provided by an academic process.

In fact, there is no independently verified evidence that any individual technique or piece of software consistently and significantly outperforms the rest in a range of circumstances.

Also, be aware that the software industry is prone to relabelling old offerings to catch the current 'hype wave'. At the moment, 'Big Data' and 'Machine Learning' are in vogue, so if you hear these words always check to make sure that you are getting something 'new'.

Always independently validate the performance claims of software using your own data and meaningful comparisons. In practice, 'fit' for your business, ease of use or other factors are more likely to be reasons to favour one piece of software over another than superior forecasting performance. Any reasonably well-designed software should be able to deliver similar levels of accuracy.

TAKEOUT

Beware of buzzwords and proprietary black box methods. Question and verify.

Be suspicious of opaque and untested 'sexy' new methods

Gartner's hype cycle

'Old' methods — Tried, Tested, Trusted, Transparent

Peak of inflated expectations

Plateau of productivity

Slope of enlightement

Trough of disillusionment

Visibility →

Time →

Black Box

'Exciting' new technology

Purchasing criteria

Stock Performance   Fit to business   Ease of use

The methods used in different software packages are not always correct

Although the overwhelming majority of forecasting algorithms used in software packages are in the public domain, you cannot assume that they have been implemented correctly.

Unfortunately, there are many examples of commercially available software with forecasting algorithms and accuracy metrics that have been poorly implemented. So, while superior forecasting performance is unlikely to be a reason to select a particular vendor, poor performance might be a reason to avoid one.

Before making a purchasing decision, take steps to independently validate the quality of the products that you are choosing from. Give them some sample data and then analyse the errors yourself – ideally based on 'value added' (see page 74).

(see page 74)

TAKEOUT

Never let vendors 'mark their own homework'. Test, don't assume.

Forecasting methods may not be the reason to buy...

... but they may be the reason not to

Most forecast models are based on the same design....

... but don't assume they have been 'engineered' to the same standards

Caveat Emptor

Validate before you buy

Autoselect algorithms do not always select the best forecasting method

Some forecasting software offers only one favoured method. Others provide a wide range (perhaps up to 100). In principle, choice is good, but in practice few forecasting practitioners completely master the technicalities of more than a handful of techniques. So, the combination of methods and tuneable parameters can make the process of choosing the best way produce a forecast bewildering.

For this reason, many software suppliers provide 'autoselection' algorithms to make the choice on behalf of forecasters.

Unlike the forecasting methods themselves, which are usually in the public domain, autoselection algorithms are usually proprietary and 'black box', so a user cannot check how they work or how good they are. Here are a few tips to make sure that this functionality is working for you:

1. Make sure that they are measuring the quality of forecasts in a 'hold out sample', not the fit of a model to history, and that the history used to generate the model and the hold out sample is large enough
2. Ensure that they are using appropriate error metrics to assess the quality of forecasts – ideally value added
3. Check whether the sample of models from which the software is selecting are the right ones for your data. For example, choosing from a selection of trended or seasonal models when demand is stationary will result in poor forecasts.
4. Independently check the error metrics that the process produces.
5. Check that the selected model replicates its 'test' performance in real life.
6. If you are able to manually influence model selection, chose a simple 'good enough' model rather than a 'perfect' complex one
7. Rerun autoselect algorithms periodically.

TAKEOUT

Make sure that 'autoselect' algorithms use accepted good practice and validate the outcome.

Auto selection helps deal with the complexity of model selection and tuning

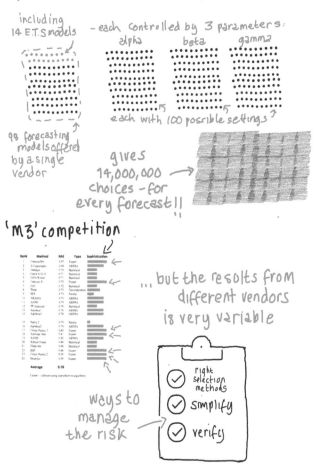

including
14 E.T.S models

98 forecasting models offered by a single vendor

- each controlled by 3 parameters:
  alpha   beta   gamma

each with 100 possible settings

gives
14,000,000
choices - for
every forecast!!

'M3' competition

Sophistication

... but the results from different vendors is very variable

Rank	Method	RAE	Type	Sophistication
1	ForecastPro	0.47	Expert	
5	3-1 automatic	0.68	ARIMA	
4	Dampen	0.70	Statistical	
5	Comb S-H-D	0.71	Statistical	
6	Delta Wmage	0.71	Statistical	
6	Theta-sm X	0.72	Expert	
7	BJF	0.72	Statistical	
8	Flode	0.72	Decomposition	
9	SES	0.73	Simple	
10	AAM1-A	0.73	ARIMA	
11	AAM1	0.74	ARIMA	
12	RF Automatic	0.74	Statistical	
13	Autobox1	0.75	ARIMA	
14	Autobox2	0.74	ARIMA	
15	Naive 2	0.75	Naive	
16	Autobox2	0.75	ARIMA	
17	Theta-Picto1	0.80	Expert	
18	Autoregr Arar	0.81	Expert	
19	AAM2	0.82	ARIMA	
20	Robust Trend	0.85	Statistical	
21	Theta-Sm	0.84	Statistical	
22	RBF	0.88	Expert	
23	Theta-Picto 2	0.89	Expert	
24	Smartfcs	0.90	Expert	
	Average	**0.79**		

Expert = software using automation algorithms

ways to manage the risk

- ✓ right selection methods
- ✓ simplify
- ✓ verify

Machine learning technology will not eliminate the need for human input into forecasting

Almost every day sees a new prediction that machine intelligence will take over the world, rendering human beings surplus to requirements. Unsurprisingly, forecasting has not been immune to this – indeed arguably since any purposeful act involves a form of forecast (if I do 'A' then 'B' will happen) the ability to forecast is a prerequisite of all machine intelligence.

So, expect the next wave of forecasting software innovation to make major claims for the benefits of AI (artificial intelligence) and machine learning.

While it is likely that the world will be transformed by these technologies there are a number of reasons why I think we can discount the more extreme vision of omniscient machines taking over forecasting.

1. The future is never like the past, and this isn't going to change (not least because of the impact of machine intelligence on the world) So, extrapolation from the past no matter how sophisticated the technology used to do it is never going to be 100% successful

2. A machine needs human beings to help it make sense of the past before it can make predictions. The algorithms behind 'self driving cars' are trained to spot the difference between papers bags blowing across a road and dogs by mimicking the judgements used by human beings. By the same token, machines cannot tell the difference between a 'one off event' and a recurring event without human input.

3. All this requires huge volumes of high quality, consistent data – something that is often in short supply in forecasting.

4. A machine will never 'know' that you (or your competitor) is about to run an advertising campaign, and what impact it is likely to have.

TAKEOUT

Be sceptical of claims that machine learning will eliminate the need for human input and judgement.

Why machine learning won't take over forecasting

Needs

Data

Lots of historical data.....

Challenges

Novelty

Discontinuity

cannot forecast change and has no....

Training

... which needs to be interpreted with human guidance

Insight

'external' knowledge e.g. based on market intelligence

Combining forecasts produces better results

It is tempting to assume that there will always be one 'best' algorithm for forecasting any particular data series.

In fact, research has consistently demonstrated that using an average forecast from a range of methods tends to outperform any single one.

The reason for this is that any single method will be successful in picking up some aspects of a signal, but not others. Also, every method will be confused by noise, but in slightly different ways.

For this reason, academics often recommend 'ensemble forecasting', and while it is used extensively in weather forecasting it is not commonly applied in demand forecasting because of the computational overhead involved.

Unless your software supports it (and some of the more sophisticated products do), using an average of methods might not be a practical approach for operational forecasters. But this does illustrate why it isn't worth expending too much effort searching for the optimum.

Instead of searching for the theoretical optimum, focus your efforts on ensuring that your forecasts are not (badly) wrong in practice. Better to be roughly right rather than precisely wrong.

> ### TAKEOUT
> Don't waste time and resources by trying to 'perfectly optimise' on one method - settle for 'good enough'.

Combine forecasts to get better results

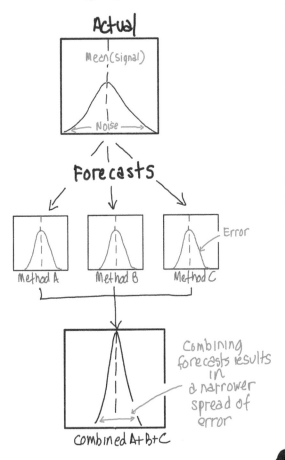

Actual

Mean (signal)

Noise

Forecasts

Method A   Method B   Method C   Error

Combined A+B+C

Combining forecasts results in a narrower spread of error

SECTION 4
UNDERSTANDING FORECAST
PERFORMANCE

Poor forecasting?
Random variation?

Advanced

'Trust but verify'
Russian Proverb

No kind of process will consistently deliver good results without a functioning feedback mechanism, as any engineer will tell you. Feedback tells you whether a system is performing as intended and provides information that enables corrective action to be taken.

Forecasting is no different to any other process in this regard, which is why measuring and interpreting forecast error (the difference between actual and forecast demand) is so important.

This section outlines how best to measure the performance of a forecast process and make sense of the results.

The measurement challenge

So here is the forecasters dilemma:

There will always be forecast error. The challenge is to work out the cause of the error and to take the appropriate action based on this knowledge. This means determining whether error is due to:

- The forecasting model being wrong - which would require it to be changed or recalibrated
- A temporary or permanent change in the behavior of the system being forecast – which might require a new model or for the existing one to be supplemented with judgement
- Noise – which cannot be changed, so the correct course of action is to do nothing

In practice, all these factors are jumbled up together and can vary enormously in size and impact.

Forecast error taken in isolation will never tell you how good a forecast is and what should be done to improve performance, because an unknown proportion of it will be unavoidable noise.

The measurement challenge is to understand ....

1. What proportion *of the error** is <u>unavoidable</u>?

Cause?		Remedy?
Noise	→	None

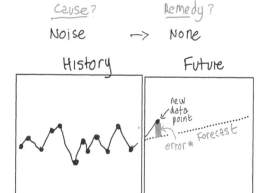

| History | Future |

new data point

Forecast

*error**

2. What proportion *of the error** *(if any)* is <u>avoidable</u>?

Cause?		Remedy?
Wrong model	→	Change model
Right model – wrong parameters	→	Adjust parameters
Poor judgement	→	Learn & change behaviour

Conventional error metrics

Forecast performance is measured by error on two dimensions: the direction of the error and the size of the error

The direction of error takes account of the error sign (i.e. positive or negative) whereas measures of the size of the error ignore it, (i.e. they use the absolute value). Both direction and size are normally expressed as a percentage (of the actual or the forecast value). Error might be measured for a single period or over a time range; for a single forecast or a set of forecasts.

An example of a direction metric is the Mean Percentage Error (MPE), which measures bias – the tendency to over forecast or under forecast. By definition, this looks at a time range, but often the error measure for a single period is incorrectly labelled 'bias'. Since forecasts will always be either too high or too low, the direction of error for a single period tells you nothing meaningful about the direction of error.

The most common 'size' metric is 'Mean Absolute Percentage Error' (MAPE), which uses the same error data as MPE but ignores the sign. MAPE has technical problems that make it unpopular with academics and experts in the field, but for practitioners its most obvious weakness is that it cannot be used to measure performance of a portfolio of forecasts. For this reason, metrics like the weighted absolute percentage error (WAPE) or forecast accuracy are also frequently used. Rather than average the errors for a single forecast over time, these measures use a weighted average of the errors for a range of forecasts for a single period.

These are the most commonly used measures, but there are scores of other ones. Also, in practice, it is rare to find even the same metric applied in a consistent manner between businesses, and sometimes even within the same one. But the biggest problem with conventional metrics is that they are a poor measure of how well forecasts fulfil their purpose – helping to make better replenishment decisions.

TAKEOUT

Be cautious when using conventional errors metrics. Many are technically flawed, calculated in inconsistent ways and none meaningfully reflect the impact of forecast performance on the business

Traditional metrics are flawed

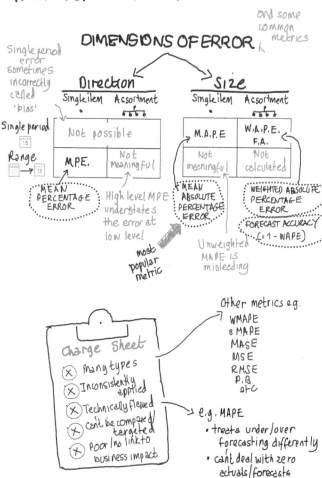

DIMENSIONS OF ERROR

and some common metrics

Single period error sometimes incorrectly called 'bias'

	Direction		Size	
	Single item	Assortment	Single item	Assortment
Single period	Not possible		M.A.P.E	W.A.P.E. F.A.
Range	M.P.E.	Not meaningful	Not meaningful	Not calculated

MEAN PERCENTAGE ERROR

High level MPE understates the error at low level

MEAN ABSOLUTE PERCENTAGE ERROR

most popular metric

Unweighted MAPE is misleading

WEIGHTED ABSOLUTE PERCENTAGE ERROR

FORECAST ACCURACY (= 1 - WAPE)

Other metrics e.g.
WMAPE
sMAPE
MASE
MSE
RMSE
P, B
etc

Charge Sheet
- (X) many types
- (X) inconsistently applied
- (X) Technically flawed
- (X) can't be compared/targeted
- (X) poor/no link to business impact

→ e.g. MAPE
- treats under/over forecasting differently
- can't deal with zero actuals/forecasts

69

Period errors are not meaningful

Many traditional forecast metrics are based on analysing results for a single period, but this approach is unlikely to provide meaningful insight.

There are two reasons for this.

First, since bias is systematic error it can only be detected by analysing a series of errors over time.

Second, often most of the errors in a single period will reflect unavoidable error. In other words, they will be mainly made up of noise rather than true forecast error, which means that measures like WAPE and Forecast Accuracy paint a misleading picture of forecast performance.

Using an average of errors over time dampens the impact of noise resulting in a more meaningful measure.

TAKEOUT

Never try to make sense of single period errors. Always analyse forecast error using an average over time.

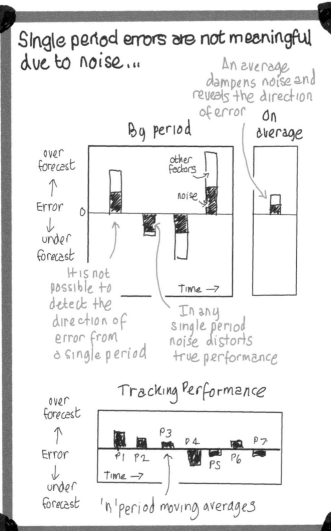

Single period errors are not meaningful due to noise...

An average dampens noise and reveals the direction of error

By period

On average

over forecast

↑

Error   0

↓

under forecast

other factors

noise

It is not possible to detect the direction of error from a single period

Time →

In any single period noise distorts true performance

Tracking Performance

over forecast

↑

Error

↓

under forecast

P1 P2 P3 P4 P5 P6 P7

Time →

'n' period moving averages

The denominator is not important

Civil wars have been fought in the practitioners' community over whether it is best to use actuals or forecasts as the denominator when calculating error percentages.

When the wrong metrics are used to measure performance in the wrong way e.g. MAPE for a single period, whether you choose forecast or actual to calculate the percentage error can make a big difference.

But correctly using average rather than single period values reduces the distortion caused by the choice of denominator.

And using error metrics that don't have the technical flaws of most conventional methods makes the issue irrelevant.

TAKEOUT

Don't waste any energy arguing about what denominator to use in calculating error percentages - in practice, if you measure it in the right way, it is irrelevant.

What to use as the denominator when calculating percentage forecast error is often the source of lively debate

	P1	P2	P3	P4	Average
Actual	1	4	3	4	3
Forecast	3	1	2	4	2.5

In a single period the choice makes a difference ...

... but when averages are used instead it becomes largely irrelevant

Value Added - the ultimate measure of forecast quality

Forecasting is not an art form. There are no marks for style or sophistication.

The only thing that matters is whether it works – that is, does it add value to a business?

Since the alternative to forecasting is to replenish stocks on a simple 'one in, one out' basis, the value added by forecasting can be measured by comparing the actual forecast error to the error that would have resulted from using the actual from the previous period as the forecast.

This is called a 'naïve forecast' for the obvious reason that it is the simplest – dumbest – alternative forecast method.

So, the ultimate measure of forecast quality is the degree to which the actual forecast error beats the naïve forecast error, on average. This is called the 'Relative Absolute Error'.

A RAE below 1.0 indicates that value is being added. Anything larger than 1.0 indicates that value is being destroyed, and that it would have been better to have replenished stock based on past demand rather than trying to forecast it.

RAE is calculated for an individual forecast, but the RAE for a portfolio can be calculated using the weighted average values.

The value that is added is ultimately manifest as lower stocks and better customer service, both of which can be valued.

Forecasting is a means to an end.
Use RAE to measure the value that it adds

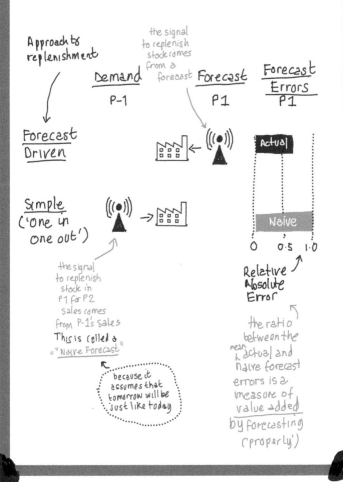

Approach to replenishment

the signal to replenish stock comes from a forecast

Demand
P-1

Forecast
P1

Forecast Errors
P1

Forecast Driven

Simple ('one in one out')

the signal to replenish stock in P1 for P2 sales comes from P-1's sales

This is called a "Naive Forecast"

because it assumes that tomorrow will be just like today

Actual

Naive

0   0.5   1.0

Relative Absolute Error

the ratio between the mean actual and naive forecast errors is a measure of value added by forecasting ('properly')

75

Forecast Value Added (FVA) - the measure of the effectiveness of steps in the forecast process

The concept of value added as measured by RAE is sometimes confused with the related idea of Forecast Value Added, as promoted by Mike Gilliland, the forecasting expert.

FVA measures the value added by different steps in the forecast process by looking at how error metrics change, like when judgement is applied to statistical forecasts, for instance.

RAE, on the other hand, measures performance compared to a hypothetical first step in the process, which is the creation of a naïve forecast. Value added using RAE is usually calculated for the whole process but can be calculated at each process step in the same way as FVA.

TAKEOUT

Use Value Added as measured by RAE and FVA. They are different but complementary approaches to measuring forecast performance

The concept of 'Value Added' is related to
- but not the same as -
'Forecast Value Added' (FVA)

Value Added

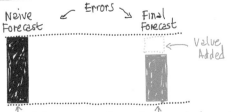

Value Added measures the difference between actual forecast performance and not forecasting

Forecast Value Added

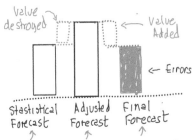

FVA measures the change in performance between steps in the forecast process

77

Some demand series are more forecastable than others

It is much easier to forecast the demand of a staple commodity, like say bread, than it is to forecast demand for a product where customers behaviour is more fickle.

But behaviour might be difficult to forecast because the product is a fashion product or because it is new, or because demand is affected by unpredictable external factors like the weather or the actions of competitors.

It is also easier to forecast demand when the data has less noise in it, perhaps because it is more aggregated.

For this reason, it is not possible to judge the quality of a forecast or the performance of a forecasters, or the method used by the size of the error alone.

All conventional error metrics, such as MAPE, are based on the size of errors and make no allowance for forecastability. This means that they can only be safely used to track the performance of a single forecast over time when we are sure that there has been no change in the pattern of demand – they cannot be used to judge or compare the quality of different forecasts.

MAPE, and other convetional error metrics, are essentially meaningless as measures of performance.

TAKEOUT

Don't use conventional errors metrics to judge the quality of forecasts as they do not allow for the forecastability of data series.

Some data series are more forecastable than others

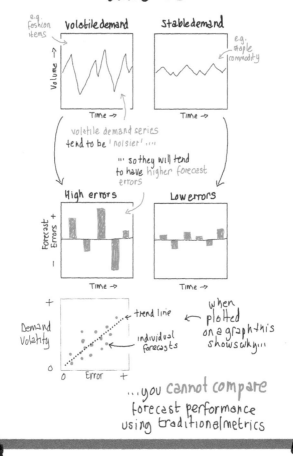

e.g. fashion items

Volatile demand

Volume →

Time →

Stable demand

e.g. staple commodity

Time →

volatile demand series tend to be 'noisier' ....

... so they will tend to have higher forecast errors

High errors

Forecast Errors
+

–

Time →

Low errors

Time →

+

Demand Volatility

0

0   Error   +

trend line

individual forecasts

when plotted on a graph this shows why...

...you **cannot compare** forecast performance using traditional metrics

Comparing to the naïve forecast
error adjusts for forecastability

Comparing the naïve forecast error to the actual error measures how much value forecasting has added to a business…or destroyed.

But comparing the actual forecast errors to those for the naïve forecast has an additional benefit.

Error has two causes: a failure to pick up and forecast the signal or noise in a data series - which is unforecastable in principle.

It is easier to forecast a stationary signal than one that changes, and stable data series are also likely to contain less noise than volatile ones, which makes them easier to forecast well, by definition. So, a good way to measure the forecastability of a data series is to measure the level of period to period changes.

Since a simple naive forecast uses the actual for one period as the forecast for the next, the naïve forecast <u>error</u> is a measure of the volatility of a data series and consequently its forecastability.

In this way, comparing actual forecasts to the naïve forecast error using the RAE not only helps us to measure value added but also allows us to compare forecast performance across many data series with different levels of forecastability.

TAKEOUT

Compare forecast errors with the naïve forecast and you get two benefits for the price of one. You measure how much value you have added compared to not forecasting AND you adjust for forecastability.

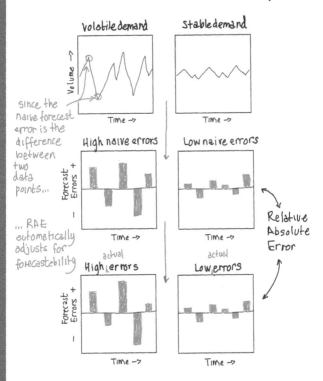

RAE measures Value Added ..
        AND allows for forecastability

Volatile demand

Stable demand

since the naive forecast error is the difference between two data points...

High naive errors

Low naive errors

Relative Absolute Error

... RAE automatically adjusts for forecastability

actual
High errors

actual
Low errors

...so you can compare forecast performance using RAE

How to quantify the level of avoidable errors - the limits of forecastability

Most people recognize that some level of error is inevitable because it is not possible to predict the future perfectly.

But it is also commonly assumed that it is not possible to determine the level of unavoidable error. Which is another way of saying that it is not possible to work out how good a forecast actually is, or how to target forecast performance

In practice, it is possible to make a good approximation of the limits of forecastability using RAE. And this means that it IS possible to make objective judgements about the quality of forecast performance.

This is because it can be proved that if a signal is stationary and noise is randomly distributed around it, the best RAE achievable is 0.7.

In real life, it is extremely unlikely that the signal is stationary, and if it were possible to predict its movement then it is possible to achieve lower RAE. The question is 'how much lower'?

In practice, because granular data series are very noisy, it is difficult to isolate how much of the period to period movement is attributable to noise and how much to the signal. This places a practical limit on how good a forecast can be, which has proved to be in the region of 0.5.

TAKEOUT

Use RAE to determine how good your forecasts are. The closer to 0.5 the better.

Use RAE to estimate the limits of forecastability

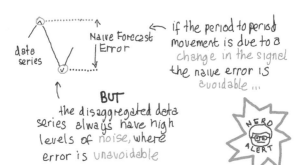

data series

Naive Forecast Error

← if the period to period movement is due to a change in the signal the naive error is avoidable ...

BUT
the disaggregated data series always have high levels of noise, where error is unavoidable

NERO ALERT

... which we can use to determine the limits of forecastability _in practice_

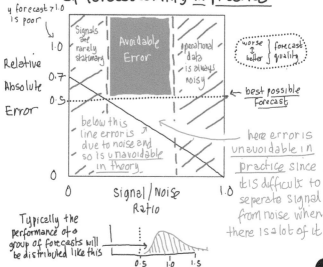

y forecast >1.0 is poor

Relative Absolute Error

1.0

0.7

0.5

0

Signals are rarely stationary

Avoidable Error

operational data is always noisy

worse ↕ better } forecast quality

← best possible forecast

below this line error is due to noise and so is unavoidable in theory

0   Signal / Noise Ratio   1.0

here error is unavoidable in practice since it is difficult to seperate signal from noise when there is a lot of it

Typically the performance of a group of forecasts will be distributed like this

0.5   1.0   1.5

83

Errors always increase over time

Forecasts are always likely to be wrong, and they usually get 'wronger' over time.

This is because the further ahead you look, the greater the chance that the real world behaviour that you are trying to forecast will change – maybe just a little, but possibly quite a lot.

This means that you cannot compare errors from forecasts that have different horizons – it is like comparing apples with pears.

An important practical consequence of this is that it makes sense to reduce your reliance on forecasts by shortening decision making lead times.

And if you are thinking of doing things that lengthen your decision-making lead times – like sourcing products from a more distant supplier - make sure that you take account of the impact of higher forecast errors on your business.

How many businesses who have outsourced their production to China because the unit cost was lower factored the impact of having to rely on less accurate forecasts into their business cases? Was the impact of higher safety stock level and the increased cost of responding to unexpected spikes in demand taken into account? Not often, I'm sure.

TAKEOUT

Don't compare errors measured over different lags. The level of error almost always increases the further out you forecast. Make sure that the impact of lead times on forecast error is factored into sourcing decisions.

Errors almost always increase with forecast lags

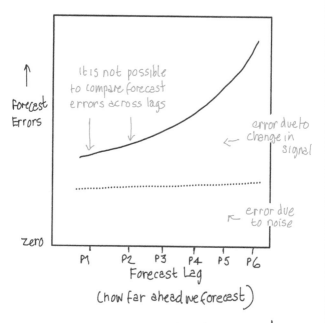

It is not possible to compare forecast errors across lags

↑

Forecast Errors

← error due to change in signal

← error due to noise

zero

P1 P2 P3 P4 P5 P6

Forecast Lag

(how far ahead we forecast)

..... so changing replenishment lead times (e.g. moving production off shore) leads to:

leading to → higher errors
leading to → higher stocks
→ higher costs

...but very often these are not factored into decision making

Allow for different lags when measuring the value added by forecasts

Take care when you are using value added measures like RAE over longer lags. They still work but they require some subtle changes to how value added is measured and interpreted.

Value added metrics like RAE capture two things:
1. Forecast performance, adjusting for the forecastability of the data series.
2. The performance of the forecast process compared to the alternative of 'simple replenishment'.

The inherent forecastability of the data series doesn't change when the forecast lag changes, but comparing forecast performance relative to the alternative of simple replenishment does need to change to reflect the longer lead time.

For example, if it takes three months from forecast to the replenishment of stock (perhaps because it comes from China), the three months out error should be compared with the naïve error from three months prior, not that for the last month.

This is called 'Lag Adjusted' value added.

Unsurprisingly, 'Lag Adjusted' value added is usually better than non 'Lag Adjusted' performance. The difference between the two reflects the penalty of longer lead times and what could be saved by shortening them.

Adjust RAE for forecasting lags

RAE measures actual forecast performance
relative to two things:

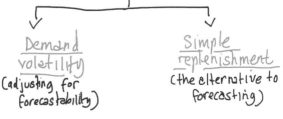

Demand
volatility
(adjusting for
forecastability)

Simple
replenishment
(the alternative to
forecasting)

These give the same
results when the
replenishment leg
is one period...

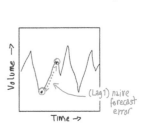

(Lag1) naive
forecast
error

Volume →

Time →

... but if the lag is greater
than one period the RAE used
for comparing performance
needs to be adjusted to
reflect this

NERD
ALERT

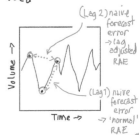

(Lag 2) naive
forecast
error
→ lag
adjusted
RAE

(Lag1) naive
forecast
error
→ 'normal'
RAE

Volume →

Time →

Bias and variation - two types of error

To properly understand and act upon value added measures it is important to differentiate between the two ways in which a forecast can be 'wrong'.

First, you might fail to identify the <u>level</u> of demand. You might consistently forecast too high or too low.

This kind of error is called BIAS

The second kind of error is if you failed to correctly identify the <u>pattern</u> of demand. An example of this kind of error would be if demand moved up from one period to the next and your forecast moved down.

This kind of error is called VARIATION.

It is important to differentiate between these two types of error because they impact the business in different ways. The often have different causes as well – which means that they need to be managed in different ways.

> TAKEOUT
> Always differentiate between bias (systematic error) and variation (unsystematic error)

Bias and variation: two types of error;
different causes ... different remedies

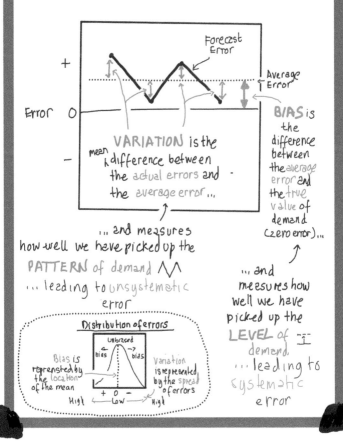

Forecast Error

Average Error

Error   0   +   −

VARIATION is the mean difference between the actual errors and the average error ...

... and measures how well we have picked up the **PATTERN** of demand ⋀⋀ ... leading to unsystematic error

BIAS is the difference between the average error and the true value of demand (zero error)...

... and measures how well we have picked up the **LEVEL** of $\bar{x}$ demand. ... leading to systematic error

Distribution of errors

Unbiased

Bias is represented by the location of the mean

Variation is represented by the spread of errors

High ← + 0 − → High
      Low

The different business impact of bias and variation

Bias and variation impact the business in different ways. Bias means that you order either too much or too little product (from suppliers or from manufacturing).

Persistent over forecasting means that you will have too much 'cycle stock' – which leads to cash being unnecessarily tied up in inventory, higher warehousing and financing costs and you run a greater risk of stock obsolescence.

But if demand has been persistently under forecast, you will have too little cycle stock, which will result in lost sales (and poor customer service) or you will incur extra costs sourcing extra supplies at short notice to meet demand.

In addition to cycle stock, most businesses hold safety stock to absorb the inevitable variation in forecast error (due to unforecastable noise and suboptimal forecasting).

The level of safety stock required is determined by the target service level and the level of variation. Higher variation will therefore lead to higher stocks, which impacts cash flow and costs in the same way as over forecasting.

But, while over forecasting and variation both increase the level of stock the size of the impact differs. One 'unit' of bias due to over forecasting will result in one unit of extra cycle stock. But one unit of additional variation will have a bigger impact because safety stock is based on a multiple of error.

Note that safety stock is only designed to absorb variation. It does not protect you from the negative consequences of persistent under forecasting (bias).

TAKEOUT

Eliminate bias to ensure that you have the right level of cycle stock. Reduce variation to keep the level of safety stock to a minimum.

The different business impact of bias and variation

Reduce BIAS to make sure there is not either too much or too little

↑ holding costs
↑ obsolescence

↑ lost sales
↑ expediting costs

→ CYCLE STOCK is ordered from suppliers based on a forecast of demand

↓ holding costs
↓ obsolescence

←·····Inventory

Reduce VARIATION to minimise the level of

→ SAFETY STOCK is a cushion that absorbs variation in errors ... ensuring that customer demand is met

Target Service Level (↑TSL ↑SS)

+ 0 —
Errors
underforecast

The causes of bias

Bias is the result of a failure to correctly forecast the <u>level</u> of demand.

It is possible that bias – persistent under or over forecasting - is the result of choosing a poor forecasting algorithm, but it is not the most likely cause.

Bias is usually the product of poorly judged or deliberately biased judgemental adjustments.

It is therefore easy – in principle - to tackle bias.

In principle, all bias is avoidable.

TAKEOUT

To reduce bias, target misjudged manual intervention in the forecast process.

Bias is most often associated with judgemental forecasting

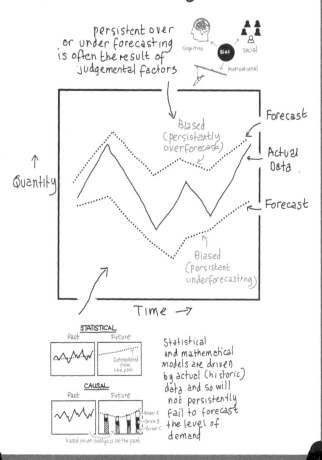

persistent over or under forecasting is often the result of judgemental factors

Cognitive   Bias   Social

Motivational

↑ Quantity

Biased (persistently overforecast)

Forecast

Actual Data

Forecast

Biased (persistent underforecasting)

Time →

STATISTICAL

Past   Future

Extrapolated from the past

CAUSAL

Past   Future

Driver A
Driver B
Driver C

based on analysis of the past

Statistical and mathematical models are driven by actual (historic) data and so will not persistently fail to forecast the level of demand

The causes of variation

Variation is the consequence of failing to pick up the <u>pattern</u> of demand.

Put simply, high variation is the result of the forecast going up when the actual data series goes down, and vice versa.

This may be the result of choosing the wrong forecast algorithm. For example, when a non-seasonal forecasting algorithm has been used when there is seasonality in the demand pattern, or vice versa. It could also be that the forecasting algorithm has been 'over-fitted', and is generating forecasts based on noise rather than a signal.

But it could also be due to poorly timed manual interventions. For example, if an uplift forecast in period 1 doesn't materialise until period 2 this would be reflected in high variation.

It is sometimes difficult to determine whether moderate levels of variation are good or not. If the ups and downs of a demand series are purely due to noise (which is unforecastable) a 'flat line' forecast may be the best possible forecast. If, on the other hand, the ups and downs are attributable to known or knowable factors, then lower levels of variation can be achieved.

Because the interpretation of variation is more complex, it is more difficult to reduce variation than bias. On the other hand, the prize is potentially greater because one unit of variation has a bigger impact on inventory than one unit of bias.

TAKEOUT

Reduce variation by targeting poor model specification or mistimed judgemental interventions.

Three complex causes of variation

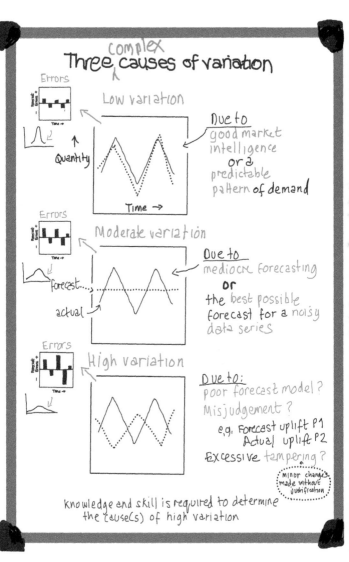

Errors

Low variation

↑ Quantity

Time →

Due to good market intelligence or a predictable pattern of demand

Errors

Moderate variation

forecast ....

actual

Due to mediocre forecasting or the best possible forecast for a noisy data series

Errors

High variation

Due to:
poor forecast model?
Misjudgement?
e.g. Forecast uplift P1
Actual uplift P2
Excessive tampering?

minor changes made without justification

knowledge and skill is required to determine the cause(s) of high variation

Conventional error metrics treat bias and variation in an inconsistent way

It makes sense to decompose total error into bias and variation – including when calculating RAE - since they have different business impacts. They also have different causes...and so need to be tackled in different ways.

But there is another reason for calculating them separately, which is that conventional error metrics can lead us to very odd conclusions.

For instance, with an intermittent demand series where more than 50% of the period values are zero, conventional error metrics tell us that the best forecast is zero...for every period!

Also, traditional metrics understate the impact of bias when the data series is volatile, and so don't reflect what we know to be the impact on cycle stock, which is independent of volatility.

The reason why we get these curious results is that traditional error metrics measure how far a forecast is away from the median of a distribution – not the mean, which is what is really important.

Always measure bias and variation separately, especially if demand series are intermittent or highly volatile.

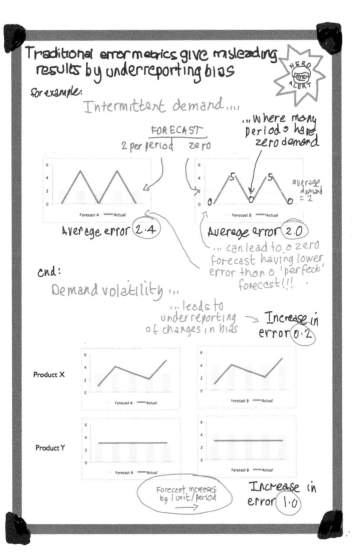

Traditional error metrics give misleading results by underreporting bias

HERO ALERT

for example:

Intermittent demand....

FORECAST
2 per period   zero

...where many periods have zero demand

Forecast A — Actual

Average error 2.4

5   5
0   0   0
Forecast B — Actual

average demand = 2

Average error 2.0

... can lead to a zero forecast having lower error than a 'perfect' forecast!!!

and:

Demand volatility ...

... leads to underreporting of changes in bias → Increase in error 0.2

Product X

Forecast A — Actual

Forecast B — Actual

Product Y

Forecast A — Actual

Forecast B — Actual

Forecast increases by 1 unit/period →

Increase in error 1.0

97

Forecasts do not need to be equally accurate across the horizon.

Not all forecasts are equal.

Your business might routinely forecast 18 months ahead but operational forecasters will only be interested in the quality of forecasts in the short-term part of this horizon.

For example, if the one month ahead forecast is used to plan production then you will be interested in ensuring that this is as reliable as possible, at the level of detail that is used to schedule production.

If raw materials need to be ordered three months in advance then the important forecast is that for the next three months, at the level of detail needed to estimate material requirements for the buyers which is likely to be different to that used to schedule production.

The most important forecast lags are those that match decision making lead times. For operational forecasters, the reliability of longer term and higher level (less detailed) forecasts are of secondary importance.

TAKEOUT

Focus attention on the forecasts used to drive key operational decisions.

Forecasts used for decision making are more important than others

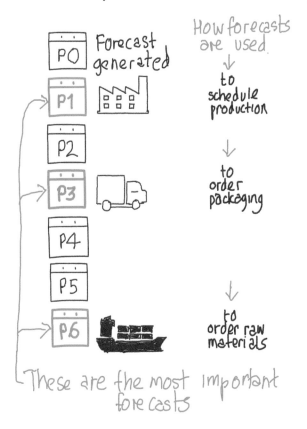

PO — Forecast generated

How forecasts are used.
↓

P1 🏭
↓
to schedule production

P2

P3 🚚
↓
to order packaging

P4

P5
↓

P6 🚢
↓
to order raw materials

These are the most important forecasts

Sometimes a forecast is not a forecast

A forecast is an estimate of an unknown future value of a variable – a best guess of what is really going to happen in the future.

We might be more confident of some elements of the future value (if there is a strong seasonal pattern for example) and less confident of others (e.g. the impact of a new product launch), but all forecasting is characterised by uncertainty.

There may be occasions when we have no uncertainty, however. A customer might make a commitment in advance, or our sales might be constrained by production capacity.

We need to remove the impact of these events from our measures of forecast quality in order not to give a misleading positive picture of forecast performance.

TAKEOUT

Remove the impact of known events from forecast measures in order to avoid giving a distorted impression of performance.

Sometimes forecasts aren't really forecasts

Customer A places
orders at the end of P1
so forecasts are required from
P2 onwards

Period 1	Period 2	Period 3

Customer A — Known demand | Forecast demand

Customer B — known demand | Forecast demand

customer B places
orders at the end
of P2 - forecasts
are only required
for P3

Period 1
NO
uncertainty
Not a
Forecast

Period 2
some
uncertainty
Partial
forecast

Period 3
uncertain
True
forecast

Because some of the demand
is known P2 'forecast' errors
will be too low.
These cannot be compared to a
true forecast

The best forecasts do not always have the lowest errors

OK, so this is getting a bit boring, but it is worth saying it one more time.

Having low forecast errors does not mean that you have got a good forecast process. It might just mean that you have a stable demand series that is easy to forecast.

Also, having high forecast errors doesn't mean that the forecasts are bad. It might mean that the demand series is highly volatile, and so difficult to forecast.

So, you cannot improve a forecast process by copying the processes used to produce 'low error' forecasts or trying to 'fix' process that produce high errors. At best this is a waste of time and effort and could even make things worse.

TAKEOUT

Don't use traditional error metrics to judge whether a forecast process is working well or badly, or to guide improvement action.

The best forecasts don't always have the lowest errors

Three different countries have very different patterns of demand for <u>the same products</u>

<u>Real data</u>

Low volatility ⟶ High volatility

Country A

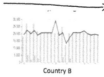

Country B

Country C

forecast average error

1	Country A	7%
2	Country B	11%
3	Country C	47%

Country A has the lowest error...

and was held up as an example for other countries to follow

average naive forecast error

1	Country C	88%
2	Country B	16%
3	Country A	6%

...but this is because the volatility of demand is very low...

Relative Absolute Error

1	Country C	0.53
2	Country B	0.70
3	Country A	1.02

...as a result it has the **WORST** forecast quality

(value destructive = worse than simple replenishment)

It is not possible to compare forecast error across levels

One thing you cannot do with ANY error metric is to compare forecasts at different levels of aggregation.

Aggregation reduces the level of noise so percentage errors calculated at a high level will always be lower than those at low level.

The same happens over time periods. Noise, and consequently forecast error measured in weekly buckets will always be higher than monthly buckets, for instance.

The same logic applies to additional data dimensions. Forecast errors measured by product AND customer will always be higher than those measured on a single dimension because the level of noise at the disaggregated level is higher.

But what is the right level at which to measure error?

Since the objective of operational forecasting is to improve supply chain performance, you should use the errors for the forecast used to make replenishment decisions – and these are usually at a low level in the product hierarchy (SKU or equivalent). Measures of the forecast quality of a portfolio should be calculated by taking the weighted average of these low-level measures.

You might want to measure errors at an even lower level (e.g. customer and SKU) to help improve forecasts, but don't use these as a measure of overall forecast performance.

TAKEOUT

Don't compare errors for forecasts made at different levels of aggregation and don't use aggregated data to measure overall forecast performance. Use errors from the level at which replenishment orders are generated and weight them to measure overall performance.

Don't compare errors from different levels

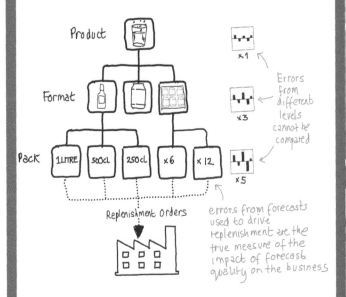

Product

Format

Pack | 1 LITRE | 500 cL | 250 cL | ×6 | ×12

×1

Errors
from
different
levels
cannot be
compared

×3

×5

Replenishment Orders

errors from forecasts
used to drive
replenishment are the
true measure of the
impact of forecast
quality on the business

MEASURING AGGREGATE PERFORMANCE

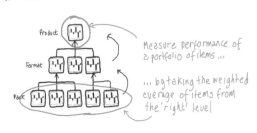

Product

Format

Pack

Measure performance of
a portfolio of items ...

... by taking the weighted
average of items from
the 'right' level

105

Error levels cannot be compared and targeted

Noise is unforecastable. Which means that there is a limit on how accurate forecasts can be.

And the level of noise can vary enormously depending on the behavior of the thing you are trying to forecast, and how aggregated your measures are.

So, you can't tell how good your forecasts are by just looking at errors in isolation, using metrics like MAPE or Forecast Accuracy.

So, if forecast A has a MAPE of 10% and forecast B 20% does that make A better than B?

You have no idea!

So, you can't compare forecast errors, and neither can you set targets for errors or forecast accuracy.

And the person who just told you that 80% forecast accuracy is good, is – to be frank – talking ****. It is simply not possible to pluck accuracy targets out of the air like this.

What you CAN say is that if my MAPE was 20% on average and its now 15% it is likely that your forecast has improved - providing that circumstances have not changed.

But that's as far as you can go with simple statements about error or accuracy.

TAKEOUT

Don't use forecast errors to target forecast performance. Use relative measures like value added (RAE) instead. Traditional error metrics can only be safely used to track the performance of a single data series over time.

You can't use traditional error metrics to compare or target different forecasts

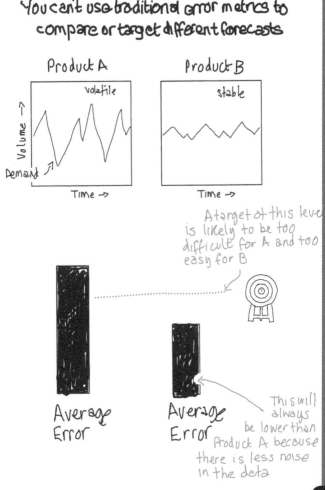

Product A

volatile

Volume →

Demand →

Time →

Product B

stable

Time →

A target at this level is likely to be too difficult for A and too easy for B

Average Error

Average Error

This will always be lower than Product A because there is less noise in the data

107

It is not impossible to benchmark forecast quality

It is not possible to compare forecast performance using traditional error metrics.

This is because of differences in the forecastability of demand series.

But it is possible to compare forecast quality using value added methods such as RAE since using the naïve forecast as a common benchmark corrects for forecastability, and also anchors the results on the business impact.

For the same reason, it is possible to benchmark performance across industries, businesses and geographies – providing you use value added methods.

Use the right metrics to compare forecast performance across industries and geographies

Product / Geography / Industry A

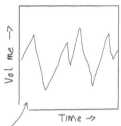

It is not possible to compare these data series using traditional metrics because of the difference in volatility

Product / Geography / Industry B

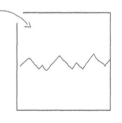

... BUT...

the naive error is largely due to noise, so using the R.A.E corrects for the difference in forecastability

Comparisons become problematical only if the volatility is due to a predictable change in the signal (e.g. seasonality / market activity)

It is not possible to measure
the quality of long term forecasts

Forecast quality can only be objectively measured in the short term – within decision making lead times.

This is because forecasts are used to inform decision making, and the decision made may in turn change future patterns of demand, so invalidating the forecast.

As a result, the difference between forecasts and actuals over the long term is often a mixture of forecast error and the results of decisions that have been made based on those forecasts, and so cannot be used to assess forecast quality.

Only short-term forecast errors – captured before any decisions made based on prior forecasts has had time to make an impact – can be used to assess forecast quality.

TAKEOUT

Only use errors within decision making lead times to assess forecast quality.

We cannot measure the quality of long term
forecasts ...

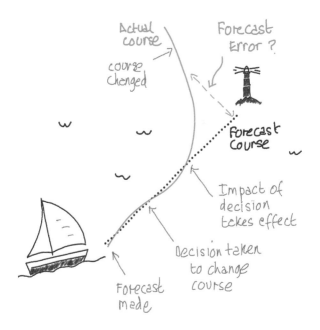

... because it is not possible to separate
true forecast error
from the
impact of decisions made
based on the forecast

Forecastability does not describe how easy it is to forecast demand

Often people confuse the concept of forecastability with the ease or difficulty of forecasting.

Sometimes volatility is difficult to forecast. Indeed, if it is entirely driven by noise it is impossible.

But some volatility is easy to forecast, when there is a regular seasonal pattern to demand or spikes are driven by well understood consumer behaviour.

It is impossible to measure the ease or difficulty of forecasting in an objective way. And even if it were, it would be irrelevant since our aim should be to maximise the value of the forecast process not measure the technical proficiency of the forecasters.

TAKEOUT

Don't attempt to measure the ease or difficulty of forecasting. It is irrelevant. Only results count - based on the value added to the business.

The difficulty or ease of forecasting cannot be measured

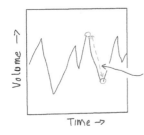

It is impossible to forecast the movement if it is due to noise...

... but we can forecast the part that is a change in the signal

BUT WE CAN NEVER KNOW

the signal to noise ratio

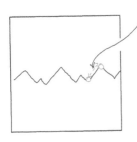

We can only infer it from our success in forecasting

CONCLUSION: it is futile to attempt to measure the difficulty of forecasting

instead

focus on the value added or destroyed

SECTION 5
MANAGING FORECAST PERFORMANCE

'Those who do not learn from their history are doomed to repeat it.'
George Santayana

Improvement in forecasting rarely follows automatically from a single act,
such as investment in software.
It comes from measuring performance, understanding why it deviates
from the achievable ideal and taking appropriate action to close the gap -
starting with the most rewarding, simplest and cheapest methods.
This section contains a series of practical suggestions of what to do, and
what not to do.

Forecast improvement is based on understanding error

There are only two ways to achieve zero forecast error.

The first is dumb luck.

The second is by deceit.

And given forecast error is inevitable we only have two choices.

Accept it.

Strive to reduce it.

And the only way to reduce error is first to determine the extent to which it was simply due to unforecastable noise. As a rule of thumb, we can say that 50% of the relative absolute error is noise, or is unforecastable for practical reasons.

If error cannot be attributed to noise we have to identify the probable cause, take action to eliminate it, and satisfy ourselves that it has worked.

All improvement comes from making mistakes and learning from them.

There are no shortcuts.

TAKEOUT

Improve forecasts by identifying the root causes of avoidable error and eliminating them.

Understand error to improve forecast performance

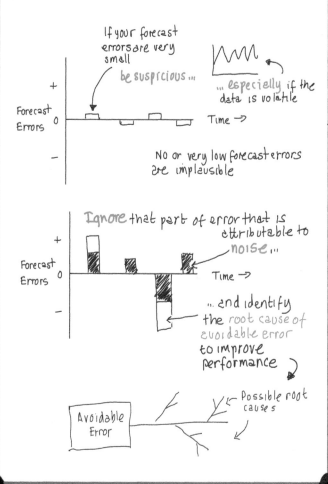

If your forecast errors are very small

be suspicious ...

... especially if the data is volatile

Forecast Errors

Time →

No or very low forecast errors are implausible

Ignore that part of error that is attributable to noise ...

Forecast Errors

Time →

... and identify the root cause of avoidable error to improve performance

Avoidable Error

Possible root causes

Forecasting is not mandatory

The objective of operational forecasting is to make better replenishment and stock holding decisions than by NOT forecasting. The alternative to forecasting is simply to replenish stock based on what has just been sold.

Simple 'one out, one in' replenishment is equivalent to using the actual for the last period as the forecast. This is called the 'naïve forecast'.

If the actual forecast error is lower than the naïve forecast error, less stock will be required than if simple replenishment were used. This is how forecasting adds value.

If the actual forecast error is higher than the naïve forecast error the forecast process has destroyed value. Typically, 30%-50% of low level forecasts destroy value.

In these circumstances, if you can't find a way of forecasting better, or the cost of doing so will outweigh the benefit, then don't. Just replenish using 'Kanban' type principles.

TAKEOUT

If you can't find a simple way of beating the naive forecast, don't try. Just replenish.

If you can't easily beat the naive forecast...

...don't try

Simple 'pull' replenishment - 'Kanban' like

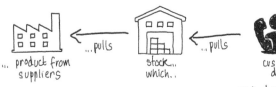

...product from suppliers ←...pulls stock... which.. ←...pulls customer demand...

...don't knock it... Toyota have built their company on this approach

works best when demand is
- not time critical
- stable
and supply is
- responsive

Forecast driven 'push' replenishment

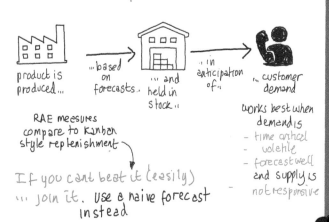

product is produced... →...based on forecasts.. ...and held in stock.. →...in anticipation of.. ...customer demand

RAE measures compare to Kanban style replenishment

If you cant beat it (easily) ... join it. Use a naive forecast instead

works best when demand is
- time critical
- volatile
- forecast well
and supply is
- not responsive

The objective should not be to increase forecast accuracy

All things being equal, it is desirable to have a lower forecast error than higher error.

But things are rarely equal.

Having a low forecast error does not necessarily mean that the forecast is good.

If a data series is relatively stable, it will tend to have low errors because it is highly forecastable. But despite having low errors the forecast can be destroying value, because the naïve forecast error will also be very low.

The objective should therefore not be to reduce absolute error but to reduce relative error. This will lead to lower stocks and so increase value added to the business.

TAKEOUT

Don't be fooled. Low errors are often associated with value destroying forecasts.

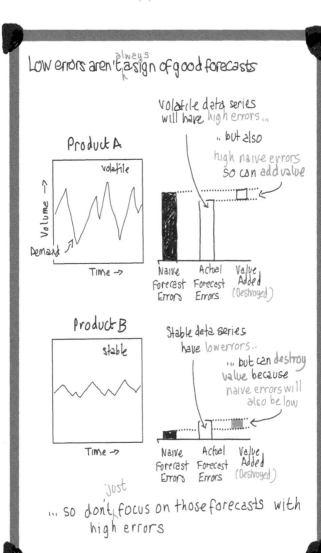

Low errors aren't always a sign of good forecasts

Product A

Volume →

volatile

Demand

Time →

Volatile data series will have high errors...

.. but also high naive errors so can add value

Naive Forecast Errors | Actual Forecast Errors | Value Added (Destroyed)

Product B

stable

Time →

Stable data series have low errors..

.. but can destroy value because naive errors will also be low

Naive Forecast Errors | Actual Forecast Errors | Value Added (Destroyed)

... so don't just focus on those forecasts with high errors

Forecasting does not always add value

People often assume that forecasting always adds value. In particular, academics have a hard time believing that a simple naïve forecast (i.e. 'same as last time') will ever consistently beat a 'proper' forecast.

In theory, they are right. Unfortunately, in practice they are wrong.

Typically, somewhere between 30% and 50% of low-level forecasts made by a business will be value destroying.

And sometimes the forecast process for a whole business or part of it is so poor – for a variety of reasons - it will destroy value in aggregate. These companies will have higher stocks and possible poorer service than if they had not forecast at all.

And usually these companies are completely ignorant of this…if they weren't, they wouldn't be investing so much time and money to make things worse.

At the other extreme, some company's forecasts add a lot of value – with errors up to 50% lower error than the naïve forecast. This should lead to a corresponding decrease in stocks, and/or improvement in customer service.

TAKEOUT

Don't rely on casual reassurances or lazy assumptions about the effectiveness of forecasting. Forecasting can add value to a business or it can destroy it. Let the measures of value added be your guide.

How value is added (or destroyed)

HOW THE SUPPLY SIGNAL IS GENERATED

SIMPLE REPLENISHMENT	FORECAST DRIVEN REPLENISHMENT
same as last period	what we anticipate next period
=	=
NAIVE FORECAST	ACTUAL FORECAST

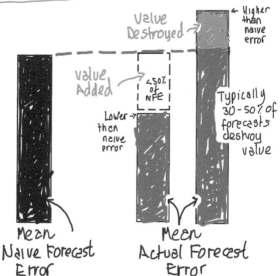

Value Destroyed →

← Higher than naive error

Value Added

↗ <50% of NFE

Lower → then naive error

Typically 30-50% of forecasts destroy value

Mean Naive Forecast Error

Mean Actual Forecast Error

Few things are unforecastable

I very frequently hear the claim that such and such types of products are 'unforecastable'.

What is usually meant by this is that the forecast errors are higher than we would like. But this isn't the same thing as being 'unforecastable'

There are only two types of data series that are truly unforecastable, in the sense that it is impossible to improve on the naïve forecast (i.e. replenishing not using conventional forecasting methods). And they don't occur in real life.

The first is where there is no signal at all. Statisticians call this a 'random walk' since the differences between the data points is the result of noise <u>and nothing else.</u>

The second is where the signal is flat and there is no noise at all. Plotted on a graph the data series is a perfectly straight horizontal line.

A data series <u>might </u>be close to one of these two extremes and this could make it uneconomic to attempt to forecast it 'properly', but the size of forecast errors is a poor guide to this. If the signal were weak, forecast errors are likely to be high, but if there was little noise the errors would be very low.

Forecast errors do not tell you whether a data series is forecastable or not. The measure of forecastability is a consistent failure to add value by beating the performance of the naïve forecast.

TAKEOUT

Don't use error measures to determine whether a data series is unforecastable. Use value added measures instead. Few data series are unforecastable in theory but many may be in practice.

Almost Everything is forecastable

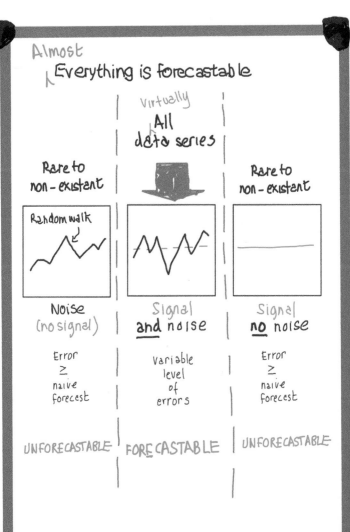

Virtually **All data series**

Rare to non-existant		Rare to non-existant
Random walk		
Noise (no signal)	Signal **and** noise	Signal **no** noise
Error $\geq$ naive forecast	Variable level of errors	Error $\geq$ naive forecast
UNFORECASTABLE	FORECASTABLE	UNFORECASTABLE

Good forecasts don't always 'look right'

Many forecasters believe that they can tell how good a forecast is by 'eyeballing' it. Good forecasts just 'look right', or so they would like to believe, which justifies them manually overriding the system generated forecast or playing around with its parameters until they get the answer they want.

In my experience 'looking right' is usually assumed to mean that the forecast must look somewhat like the past. But this is completely false.

The reason for this is that the past will contain noise but a good forecast will only be made up of a signal, and so may well look completely different. So, good forecasts will be those that DO NOT look like the past. They will look unnatural because they are unnatural – they don't have the 'rough' look that we recognise in nature. Good forecasts usually do not look 'wiggly'.

This is most clearly illustrated when we have a stable signal which is accompanied by a lot of noise.

I know of software vendors who have lost sales because prospective customers don't believe that a straight line is the best forecast possible. 'I'm not paying you for that!', they said. Also, forecasters often tamper with system generated forecasts that they 'don't like the look of' by making manual adjustments by playing around with system parameters.

There is only one exception to the rule that 'good forecasts don't have to look right'. It is sometimes helpful to look at the results of low level forecasts in aggregate. At a high level noise is damped down so visual inspection is a more reliable guide. If low level forecasts in aggregate show trends that are inconsistent with the past a demand manager should satisfy herself that there is good reason for this.

TAKEOUT

Don't judge forecasts on the basis of whether they 'look like the past'. Good forecasts will probably look very different since they discount the noise in the historic record.

Good forecasts don't always 'look right'

Low level forecasts   e.g. pack

Actual

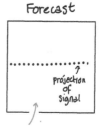

Forecast

Forecasts don't look 'natural'...
... because they have no noise-they
are 'unnatural'

Aggregated low level forecasts   e.g multiple packs

Forecast

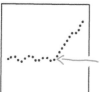

Aggregation dampens
noise so if you see...
an 'unnatural' discontinuity
like this...
... make sure there is
a good reason

127

Reacting to noise makes things worse

Forecast error always includes noise, and noise is by definition unforecastable. And if you react to the noise in the error AS IF it represented a failure in forecasting method, the likelihood is that you will make matters worse.

- You will reward – and punish – the wrong people

- You will adjust your forecast when you should leave it alone and this will make things worse

- You will waste time and effort chasing shadows

TAKEOUT

Only take action when you have sufficiently sound statistical evidence for a problem. Reacting to noise as if it were the signal will make matters worse.

How reacting to noise makes things worse

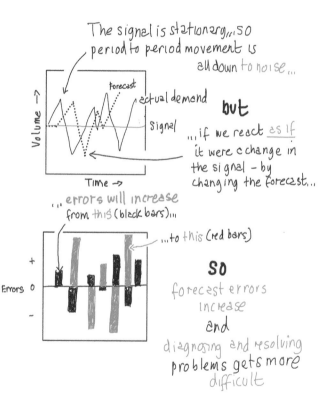

The signal is stationary... so period to period movement is all down to noise...

Forecast

actual demand

Signal

Volume →

Time →

but

...if we react _as if_ it were a change in the signal - by changing the forecast...

... errors will increase from this (black bars)...

...to this (red bars)

Errors 0
+
-

SO

forecast errors increase

and

diagnosing and resolving problems gets more difficult

this is called TAMPERING

Focussing on the biggest errors is not the best way to improve forecast quality

'Every month we ask each demand manager to identify their 'top three' forecast errors and explain what they are doing to prevent their recurrence'.

Who could possibly object to such a sensible approach? In fact, it is dead wrong – for three reasons.

First, there will always be 'a top three' forecast errors, no matter how good or bad the process. The top three could represent three forecasts that are at the limit of what can possibly be achieved and incapable of being improved.

More likely, the top three will be the tip of an ugly iceberg produced by a misfiring forecast process. This is the root cause of the problem, and this should be the focus of attention not the superficial symptoms represented by the 'top three'

Second, ask yourself what kind of forecasts will appear in the 'top three'?

They will almost certainly be the largest and most volatile products. This where you will always find the largest errors irrespective of the real quality of the forecasts.

The real villains – which may never appear on these 'most wanted' lists - could be forecasts of stable products, or lower volumes lines, where poor forecasting will never lead to large absolute errors.

Finally, there will always be exceptional unpredictable events that generate large errors, and these tend to dominate such a list. You can't improve your predication of unpredictable events, you can only improve processes that predictably generate unnecessary errors.

TAKEOUT

Don't try to improve forecasts by focussing on the 'worse offenders'. At best, it is a distracting waste of time but it can contribute to making things worse.

Why it is wrong to focus on big 'single period' errors

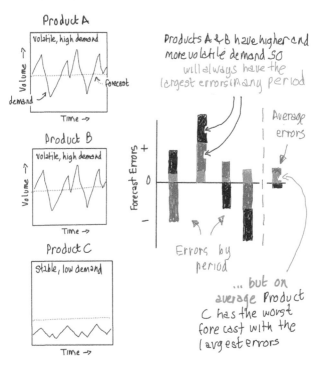

Product A

Volatile, high demand

Volume →
demand
forecast
Time →

Products A & B have higher and more volatile demand so will always have the largest errors in any period

Product B

Volatile, high demand

Volume →
Time →

Forecast Errors
+
0
−

Average errors

Errors by period

Product C

Stable, low demand

Time →

... but on average Product C has the worst forecast with the largest errors

Never rank errors by size in a single period...
this simply encourages TAMPERING

You can only measure and manage forecast error trends

Because there will always be noise in actual data, and noise is unforecastable, it is not possible to make sense of forecast errors in any single period.

The only way that you can make sense of things is by looking at the pattern of errors over time – the average level of error and the spread around the average – using statistical logic.

It is pointless to attempt to understand error for a single period. You might be able to come up with a good story but in large part you are really just 'explaining' noise.

For example, car insurers rely on the fact that the level of accidents is predictable statistically. While there might be a good reason why X crashed into Y on a particular day, this doesn't tell you anything meaningful about accidents that you can use to set premiums.

You also cannot rank or compare forecast errors for a single period. The ones near the top are probably the ones with the noisiest data series. It says nothing about the quality of the forecasts.

TAKEOUT

Always track the average errors over time. The existence of noise makes it impossible to make sense of forecast errors for a single period.

Use error trends to understand forecast performance

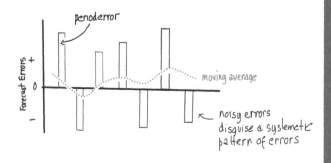

period error

Forecast Errors

+

0

−

moving average

← noisy errors
disguise a systemetic
pattern of errors

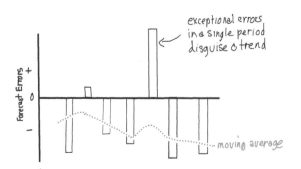

exceptional errors
in a single period
disguise a trend

Forecast Errors

+

0

−

moving average

Use moving averages to dampen the impact
of noise and help identify trends.

Improving short term forecasts is not always worthwhile

It is a common misconception that any improvement you make to forecast quality is beneficial.

An improvement to a forecast only has value if there the supply chain is able to respond to it, which may not be possible in a cost-effective way.

For example, let's assume that a business has to lock down it's replenishment orders one week before the due delivery date.

Making improvements to forecast quality within that one week 'frozen' forecast horizon – as so called 'Demand Sensing' methods aim to do – has no value since the business does not have the ability to respond to this new information.

It may be possible to expedite orders or shorten lead times, but these have cost implications that need to be offset against the benefits that better short-term forecasts can deliver.

Any unforecast demand within the frozen period will be recognised as a matter of course (as a forecast error) and may be used to inform or improve forecasts the next time that they are run. As a result there may be no value in 'sensing' demand any more quickly.

> TAKEOUT
> Don't bother trying to improve forecast quality within product replenishment lead times unless you have the ability and willingness to shorten them.

Improving forecasts can ~~be~~ sometimes be a wasted effort

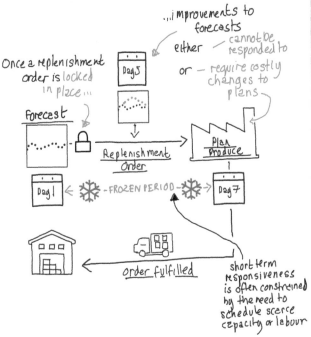

Once a replenishment order is locked in place...

Forecast

Day 5

...improvements to forecasts
either — cannot be responded to
or — require costly changes to plans

Replenishment Order

Plan Produce

Day 1 ← ❄ -FROZEN PERIOD- ❄ → Day 7

order fulfilled

short term responsiveness is often constrained by the need to schedule scarce capacity or labour

Conclusion

Changes made to forecasts within the frozen period often have no practical value

Judgemental forecasts are not always bad or always good

I find debates about whether the use of judgement in forecasting is a good or a bad thing boring and a waste of time.

If it is done well it is a good thing. If it is done badly it is a bad thing.

Instead the questions we should be asking are:

- To what extent are demand patterns predictable from the past?

- If they are not, do I have the knowledge that enables me to improve on a system generated forecast?

- How successful have my interventions been?

- Is the extra effort involved to improve my forecasts worthwhile?

TAKEOUT

Don't assume that judgement - or any other forecast method - is inherently 'good' or 'bad'. It is entirely a question of how well it is applied and whether the benefits outweigh the costs.

Judgement is not inherently good or bad

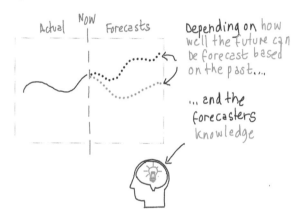

Actual | NOW | Forecasts

Depending on how well the future can be forecast based on the past....

... and the forecasters knowledge

...using judgement can either

destroy or add value...

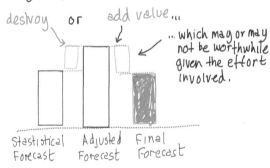

... which may or may not be worthwhile given the effort involved.

Statistical Forecast | Adjusted Forecast | Final Forecast

Forecast Value Added analysis is helps us to use judgement wisely

Consensus forecasting is not (necessarily) 'best practice'

Consensus forecasting – where forecasts are discussed and agreed in a review meeting – are sometimes promoted as 'best practice'.

It is good for decision makers to understand more about the assumptions on which forecasts are based. And even better if the consensus meeting provides a forum for people to contribute relevant knowledge to improve the forecast.

But if these meetings become a forum for different parties to negotiate mutually acceptable forecast numbers that demand managers are then required to force back into their systems, achieving 'consensus' is positively harmful.

The antidote is to assess whether, when and where such meetings add value to forecasts by measuring forecast quality 'before' and 'after'. Give forecasters the power to choose which suggestions to adopt, and hold them accountable for the results.

TAKEOUT

Use review meetings to share knowledge, not negotiate forecast numbers. Stop any practice which does not add value to the forecast process.

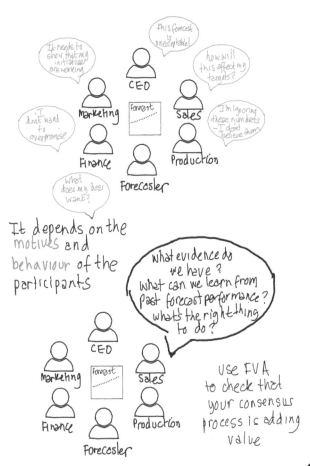

Experts are (often) no better at forecasting than non-experts

Do experts produce better forecasts than non-experts?

Research suggests that this is often not the case. This is because they are likely to place greater value on their (hard acquired) knowledge than disconfirming facts or the objective evidence of their performance.

This applies to market experts – who believe they know how customers behave, for example – and forecasting experts who believe in the power of their methods.

When your status or sense of self-worth is tied to 'being right' it is difficult to accept evidence to the contrary.

Good forecasting is based on collecting evidence about performance, interpreting it correctly and acting appropriately. This is the most valuable expertise, which 'experts' may or may not have.

TAKEOUT

Use experts where they can add value to forecasts. Where they don't, employ non experts who know how to interpret and act on evidence.

Experts can't be relied upon to make the best forecasts

they can be like hedgehogs that know one thing very well ...

Blah blah blah blah blah blah....

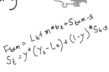

$$F_{t+n} = L_t + n*b_t + S_{t+n-s}$$
$$S_t = y*(Y_t - L_t) + (1-y)*S_{t-s}$$

... and inclined to reject anything that doesn't fit with their worldview ...

... unlike non-experts who are like foxes who seek help wherever it is available

evidence

The level of aggregation affects the ease of forecasting

The characteristics of a data series is influenced by the way it is measured.

It might make sense to break a data series into its constituent parts if they have different patterns of behaviour that are best forecast separately. For example, forecasting demand by geography or by customer might make sense if their behaviour patterns significantly differ.

However, the benefits gained by forecasting at a more disaggregated level need to be offset against the fact that they are likely to contain more noise and a weaker signal that is harder for statistical methods to pick up.

And ultimately any data series, as it is broken down into smaller and smaller measurement 'buckets', will become intermittent, at which point forecasting becomes much more challenging.

Choosing the right level at which to forecast is a key decision in the design of a forecast process since the increased insight that detailed information may provide is often wiped out by the impact of higher levels of noise in the data. The choice is a purely practical one – what works best.

TAKEOUT for the level of aggregation affects
Base your decision on the level at which you forecast based an understanding of the patterns of demand and hard evidence about what works best.

How to choose the right level to forecast at

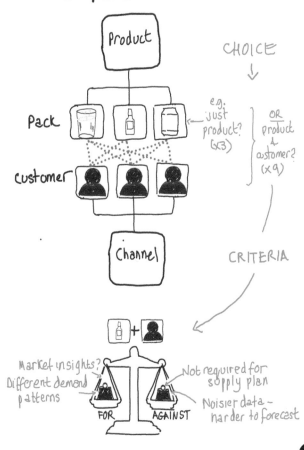

When to use 'top down' and 'bottom up' forecasting methods

Traditionally operational forecasting is conducted a low level using a 'bottom up' process. But low level granular data is much noisier than higher level data and so is more difficult to forecast – all other things being equal.

As a result, it may make sense to forecast 'top down', starting with a forecast made at a higher level that is subsequently broken down to a low level based on a formula. But this runs the risk of missing patterns in low level data that are not visible once they are aggregated.

Which approach is best to use when?

Low level forecasting will tend to work best when the behaviour of data series are very different from each other (i.e. 'independent') and the method used – whether mathematical or judgement – is good at picking these patterns up.

High level forecasting works best when the behaviour of low level items is highly correlated, and the relationship between them is stable. So, if selling more of A leads to predictably higher (or lower) sales of B then it might be best to forecast at a high level and apportion it to lower levels based on a fixed formula (e.g. pro rata to actual volume).

Forecasters often face this challenge when deciding whether to forecast product demand by customer. For replenishment purposes customer level forecasts are not required, but individual customers may behave very differently, which makes high level statistical forecasting less reliable.

In practice, a hybrid approach may the right way to go, for example forecasting at the most granular level only for those customers with more predictable behaviour.

The only way to be sure what is the best thing to do is to run a test.

TAKEOUT
Forecast 'top down' when the behaviour of low level data series is synchronized and consistent. 'Bottom up' is best when low level behaviour is very variable.

'Top down' or 'bottom up'?

Forecasting
'top down'
can work
well

... but better
to forecast
bottom up ...

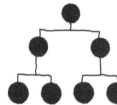

... when you
<u>know</u>
low level
that demand
patterns
are similar ...

... or you suspect
that they might
not be

usual
method

if in doubt try both and
compare the results

To disaggregate or aggregate?

If product is supplied or produced say, each week, but forecasts are produced in monthly buckets it is tempting to assume that it would be better to forecast in more detail, and more frequently, to match the cadence of the supply planning process.

All other things being equal this would be true. But unfortunately, they are not.

Forecasting at a more granular level – say weekly – enables changes in the signal within the month to be detected, which is good. But the weekly data used to generate the forecast will contain more noise than monthly buckets and so mathematical models are likely to be less accurate.

The question is will you gain more on the signal change 'swings' than you lose on the confusing noise 'roundabouts'?

As a rule of thumb, if the weekly split of sales is stable from period to period or year on year, or if the supply chain is not capable of reacting to changes to the forecast within a month, there is little to be gained from forecasting in more detail.

If the weekly split changes significantly from month to month in a way that can be forecast, and the supply chain can react, there may be some benefit for higher granularity.

The only way to find out for sure is to test both approaches and see which produces the best results.

In practice, if there is more than one driver of demand, the best approach may be a hybrid of the two. For example, perhaps forecasting 'base demand' in monthly buckets and promotional demand at a weekly level might be the way to go.

TAKEOUT

Forecast using smaller buckets when the 'within period' demand signal is unstable in a way that is capable of being forecast and if the supply chain is capable of reacting to short notice changes.

When to aggregate or disaggregate time buckets

Consistent 'in period' demand pattern

P1 P2 P3 P4

Forecast in aggregate

Inconsistent 'in period' patterns

P1 P2 P3 P4

Forecast in smaller buckets...

...providing

the changes are predictable

the supply chain can react

If in doubt try both and compare the results

Why we clean history and when to do it

Statistical forecasting methods extrapolate from history. One of the trickiest things to decide is whether the data you have gathered about the past is representative of what might happen in the future.

If it isn't representative, how do you identify significant non-recurring events that should be cleaned from the history? And how do you make sure that you remove just the incremental impact of the event?

For example, if 70% of your sales are associated with some sort of promotion, each of which is unique in the detail of its execution, are promotions 'normal business' that should be left in the history? Or is each one an exceptional event that needs to be removed? If you choose to clean history of them all, your statistical forecast is being driven by only 30% of the historical volume – all of which is highly dependent on the judgement you made about the size of the adjustments.

Given that virtually all mathematical forecasting methods are based on the assumption of having a sound historical record with which to work, it is surprising that there is so little guidance given to forecasters on this topic.

One approach is to not to cleanse history at all. Simply identify potential 'events' and buy software that enables you to model them mathematically. But this approach is out of the reach of most businesses and is built on some heroic assumptions.

Given that there is little theoretical guidance, my advice is thoroughly pragmatic.

Where an event is obviously 'one-off' (e.g. gaining or losing a customer) always adjust history. Otherwise, only touch history when there is a very large spike (or dip) in the pattern of demand that you know is abnormal and that cannot be built into a model. Track the results and adjust your approach accordingly.

TAKEOUT

Limit adjustments to history as much as possible and learn from the results. Adjusting history is unavoidable but there is no 'right way' to do it.

To cleanse or not to cleanse?

When 'cleaning' history to remove 'non recurring' events, whether to...

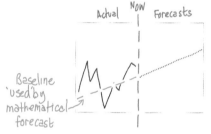

Actual | NOW | Forecasts

Baseline 'used' by mathematical forecast

... limit intervention but risk forecasts being distorted by 'one off' events or...

Actual | NOW | Forecasts

Data removed/added to history

New artificial baseline created by data cleansing

Data added to mathematical forecast

... use judgement to adjust history and shape future forecasts...

... creating extra work and most of losing the potential of mathematics

If in doubt ... don't

Judgement and when to use it

There are basically two times that you need to use judgement, in forecasting the future:

1. When there is no alternative because there is no history that you can use to build a model
2. When the history you have used to build a model includes something that needs to be removed, or excludes something that needs to be included.

Examples of the first case include new products or customers.

Examples of the second kind include when non-recurring events have been excluded from history and new non-recurring events need to be added back in (e.g. the impact of an advertising campaign) or excluded (e.g. losing a customer).

There will be occasions when a system generated forecast doesn't 'look right' and it is tempting for forecasters to manually adjust the forecast, or worse, tamper with the parameters of the model generating the forecast to get the 'right answer'. This type of judgemental intervention is potentially the most damaging because the interference in the process is hidden and will have ramifications that extend beyond the current forecast cycle.

Override or adjust system generated forecasts when you have knowledge or market intelligence that is not available to the system. And measure the effectiveness of these interventions (the 'value added') and learn.

Only adjust forecast models when you have evidence that they are not performing as they should, not on a hunch.

TAKEOUT

Don't adjust forecasts on a hunch and never manipulate forecasting models to come up with 'the right answer'. Only make adjustments when you have knowledge that the system generating the system does not have.

When to use judgement

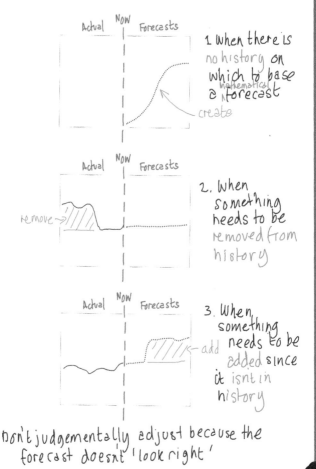

Actual | NOW | Forecasts

1 When there is no history on which to base a mathematical forecast

create

Actual | NOW | Forecasts

remove →

2. When something needs to be removed from history

Actual | NOW | Forecasts

← add

3. When something needs to be added since it isnt in history

Don't judgementally adjust because the forecast doesn't 'look right'

More frequent re-forecasting is not (necessarily) better

There are obvious advantages to forecasting more frequently and for using smaller time buckets.

For example, moving from monthly to weekly forecasts creates the opportunity to schedule replenishment more precisely and respond more quickly to changes in demand.

But before you take this step you need to ensure that your manufacturing plants and suppliers are capable of responding to changes in the forecast at a reasonable cost.

Also, you need to ensure that the additional volatility that this will inject into the supply chain is 'good volatility' – that is, it reflects changes in the demand signal and not noise.

For example, models that extrapolate from the past will respond to every single change in the data series, sometimes in an exaggerated fashion, depending on the sensitivity of the model. As a result, forecast demand (and replenishment orders) will become more volatile, making sensible planning more difficult.

It is not uncommon to find forecasts moving by over 50% from one period to the next as forecasters chase spurious accuracy at the expense of forecast stability.

Avoid this by damping down small changes, particularly for non-critical products.

TAKEOUT

Make sure that the benefits of outweigh the costs of less forecast stability before increasing the frequency of forecasting. Find ways to dampen down the forecast volatility that is attributable to noise.

Reforecasting: how more can be less (useful)

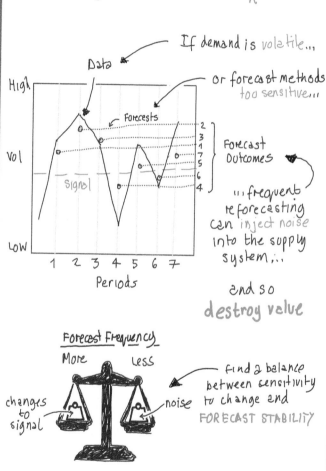

If demand is volatile...

or forecast methods too sensitive...

Data

High

Vol

Low

Signal

Forecasts

Forecast Outcomes

2
3
1
7
5
6
4

...frequent reforecasting can inject noise into the supply system...

1 2 3 4 5 6 7
Periods

and so **destroy value**

Forecast Frequency

More   Less

changes to signal   noise

find a balance between sensitivity to change and FORECAST STABILITY

Segment the product portfolio to get better results

Not all forecasts are equal, and neither are forecasting methods.

Different methods work more or less well depending on the nature of the demand signal and the level of noise. Segmenting the portfolio based on the characteristics of the demand series makes it easier to apply the correct kind of methods.

If the demand signal is stable, simple methods will often work best.

If there is a stable, signal and little noise the naïve forecast can be hard to beat. But if there is a high level of noise, choose a method that filters it out, such as a simple moving averages or single exponential smoothing.

More complex patterns such as trends or seasonal behaviour will demand more sophisticated methods. But if the demand signal is erratic, overlaying judgement on a statistical method may work best if forecasters have some understanding of what is driving this behaviour.

And always separate out intermittent demand series since they need a specialist set of forecasting methods.

Segmentation should also take account of the size of the potential prize. Only use complex or time-consuming methods (judgement) when the benefits are likely to outweigh the cost.

There is little to be gained from finessing the forecasts for low value non-critical items, so forecast them using the simplest methods possible, or simply replenish them using Kanban principles.

> ### TAKEOUT
> Segment the product portfolio to simplify the process of selecting the right method and keep the cost of the process down.

Segment your product portfolio to help select the best forecasting method

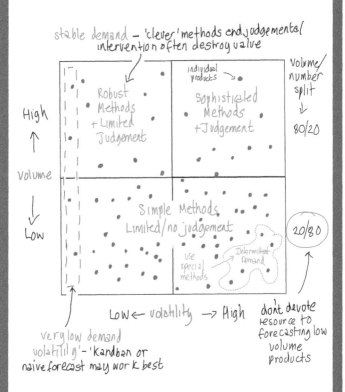

stable demand – 'clever' methods and judgemental intervention often destroy value

individual products

Volume/ number split ↓ 80/20

High ↑ Volume ↓ Low

Robust Methods + Limited Judgement

Sophisticated Methods + Judgement

Simple Methods Limited/no judgement

use special methods

Intermittent Demand

20/80

Low ← volatility → High

very low demand volatility' – 'kandban or naive forecast may work best

don't devote resource to forecasting low volume products

Standard deviation is not the way to measure volatility

Often, traditional standard deviation (SD) metrics – or variants on it like the Coefficient of Variation (COV) - are used to measure the volatility of demand series, and by implication the difficulty of forecasting them.

SD measures variation around the mean of a data series. In other words, it looks at the characteristics of the <u>population</u> of data points. The sequence in which the data arrives is irrelevant.

This means that data series that look very different can have the same SD.

But forecasters are more interested in the volatility of a data series from one period to the next, because it is this that determines how difficult or easy it is to forecast the next data point(s). Forecasters are interested in the <u>sequence</u> of data.

Instead, use the variation of the (one period ahead) naïve forecast error to measure volatility to analyse the characteristics of data series. This is mathematically related to SD but, in some circumstances, will give very different results.

TAKEOUT

Never use standard deviation to measure the volatility of demand series for forecasting purposes. Use the variation of the naïve forecast error instead.

The problem with standard deviation

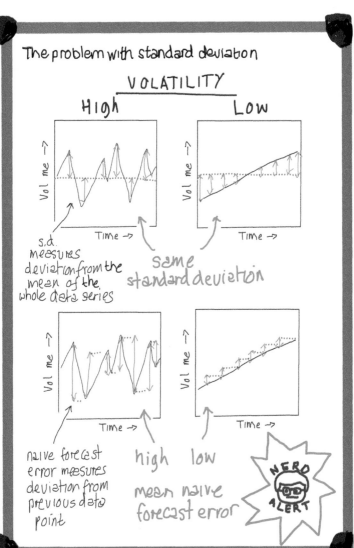

VOLATILITY

High

Volume →

Time →

s.d. measures deviation from the mean of the whole data series

Low

Volume →

Time →

same standard deviation

Volume →

Time →

naive forecast error measures deviation from previous data point

Volume →

Time →

high   low

mean naive forecast error

NERD ALERT

Better forecasts do not automatically generate business benefit

Better forecasts do not generate business benefit by themselves. Benefits only arise when forecasts are used to make better business decisions.

In practice, short term demand forecasts are used by supply planners to determine what to requisition from manufacturing or suppliers.

Unfortunately supply planners frequently ignore or adjust forecasts made by demand planners, which is likely to destroy any value added by the forecast process.

But supply planners have a second use for forecasts, since errors should be used to calculate what level of safety stocks are needed.

Often, however, rather than using the standard deviation of errors and customer service targets to set safety stock, crude methods such as days cover are used. Or safety stock is set correctly at a point in time but reviewed too infrequently, which means that improvements in forecasting have no business impact.

Even automated stock optimisation packages sometimes fail to properly apply forecast data. Some incorrectly use the variation of demand to set safety stock or fail to correctly adjust for forecasting lags or to eliminate bias from the error statistics.

TAKEOUT

Make sure demand and supply managers understand and trust each other's process to ensure that value added by the forecast process leads to better business decisions and generate business benefits.

Good forecasts don't always lead to business benefits

— links in the supply chain can break

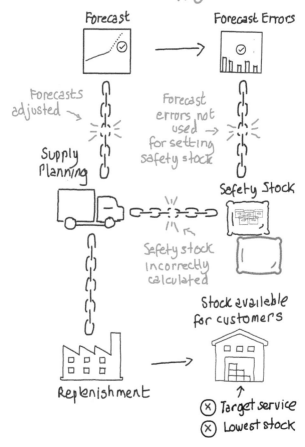

Forecast

Forecast Errors

Forecasts adjusted →

Forecast errors not used → for setting safety stock

Supply Planning

Safety Stock

Safety stock incorrectly calculated

Stock available for customers

Replenishment

(✗) Target service
(✗) Lowest stock

A business should always have 'one set of forecast numbers'

Over recent years there has been – quite rightly – a drive to using 'one set of (forecast) numbers' in businesses. It is obviously desirable that the people planning operations, finance and sales share knowledge and are working with the same set of assumptions about the future.

Unfortunately, in practice bad business forecasting habits can 'leak into' the operational forecasting process, where the impact of poor forecasting is more obvious and immediate.

For example, sales people might want to inflate forecasts to reassure their bosses that they will hit their targets or to ensure that there is product for their customers. Or finance people might want to deflate forecasts to 'manage expectations' or to create a resource buffer to help manage financial risk.

When this happens, the business is left with too much or too little stock and the finger of blame is often pointed at the demand managers.

In order to insulate operational forecasts from this bias infection, ensure that short term operational forecasts can only be adjusted by demand managers and that their independence is guaranteed. As a result, in the short term, operational forecasts are more likely to be the source of the 'one set of numbers'.

In the medium term, 'business forecasts' may be more reliable because they tend to be produced at a higher level and they are used to shape the action plans upon which forecasting assumptions are based.

No forecast should ever be artificially forced to come back to a target.

TAKEOUT

Strive for 'one (master) set of forecast numbers', but make sure that you don't import bad 'bias generating' behaviour into operational forecasts in the process.

One set of ~~forecast~~ numbers is the goal
— done the right way

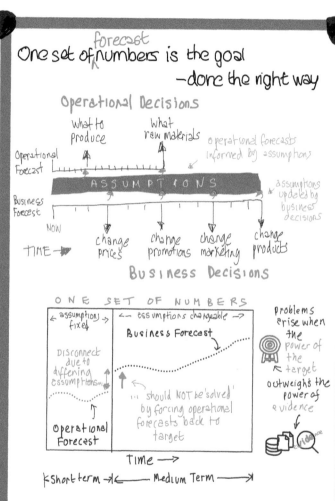

Operational Decisions

What to produce

What raw materials

Operational Forecast

operational forecasts informed by assumptions

ASSUMPTIONS

assumptions updated by business decisions

Business Forecast

NOW

TIME →

change prices

change promotions

change marketing

change products

Business Decisions

ONE SET OF NUMBERS

← assumptions fixed →

← assumptions changeable →

Business Forecast

Disconnect due to differing assumptions...

... should NOT be 'solved' by forcing operational forecasts back to target

Operational Forecast

Time →

← Short term → ← Medium Term →

Problems arise when the power of the target outweighs the power of evidence

Align assumptions and plans to align numbers

The forecast numbers do not always need to be the same

Having 'one set of (forecast) numbers' doesn't mean that short term operational forecasts and medium-term business forecasts are perfectly synchronised all the time and across all their horizons.

To fulfil their purpose, operational forecasts need to be very detailed, refreshed very frequently and be as accurate as possible. And they are most likely to contribute to the 'one set of numbers' for the short term horizon.

Business forecasts, on the other hand, need less detail, do not need to be reviewed as often and need only to be 'good enough' to make reasonable high-level resource allocation decisions. These are more likely to be the source of the 'one set of numbers' for the business in the medium term horizon.

If these two types of forecast were to be produced in exactly the same way and kept perfectly synchronised at all times over the entire horizon, they would either be too detailed or not detailed enough. Too frequent or not frequent enough; too precise or not precise enough.

As a result, produce short and medium-term forecasts using the method that is most appropriate for their differing purposes…but using the same consistent set of assumptions.

But don't try to create one forecast in one way for both purposes or two forecasts kept in perfect synchronisation at all times over the entire horizon. Just create 'touch points' at key decision making lags and certain levels in data hierarchies to make sure that the two sets of forecasts stay aligned enough to ensure that decision making in the business is properly co-ordinated.

> ### TAKEOUT
> Ensure that operational and medium-term forecasts are aligned…they don't need to be perfectly synchronised.

One set of numbers doesn't mean everything is the same all the time

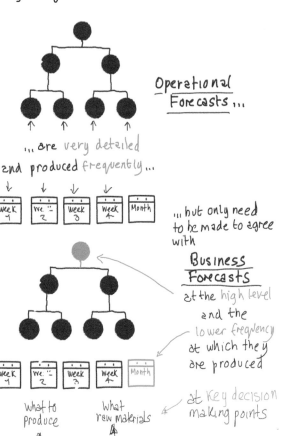

Operational
Forecasts ...

... are very detailed
and produced frequently ...

... but only need
to be made to agree
with

Business
Forecasts
at the high level
and the
lower frequency
at which they
are produced

at key decision
making points

what to
produce

what
raw materials

It doesn't matter who forecasters report to - providing...

'Where should forecasting report to?' is probably the most often asked question on forecasting blogs, but the one that is most difficult to answer... because it is the wrong question.

The reason is clear if we consider the list of desirable attributes for the forecasting role:

1. Forecasters should be numerate and have the technical capability to understand the models they use.
2. Forecasters should have domain knowledge, which may involve being close to marketing and selling.
3. Forecasters should understand and be able to influence how the numbers they produce are used to make replenishment, inventory and capacity planning decisions, which may involve them being close to supply planning.
4. Forecasting is evidence based, so forecasters need to be insulated from political pressure of all sorts.
5. Forecasters need to have access to decision makers and good communication and influencing skills, based on broad business knowledge.

In practice, it is impossible to fulfil all these requirements by engineering an organisation chart. But this doesn't stop people trying, and it is not uncommon to see forecasting flip-flopping between functions based on the whims of opinion and fashion.

Instead, make sure that the right balance is struck between these competing demands wherever the forecasting role sits in the organisation, based on an understanding of the needs of your particular business at a particular time. It is only necessary to change reporting lines if it proves impossible to adequately meet these requirements with the current organisational configuration - based on measured performance and other evidence.

TAKEOUT

Don't try to fix forecast performance by changing the organisation chart. Instead, identify and eliminate deficiencies in the current process 'in situ' wherever possible.

Good forecasting relies on a balance between ...

Good market intelligence

Numeracy and technical skills

Freedom from political interference

Ability to influence

Understanding the impact on supply

... not on the function that forecasters report to...

(which will vary with circumstances)

TERMINOLOGY

Algorithm	A mathematical procedure
Autoselection	A software routine that automatically selects those forecasting models with the lowest forecast errors
Bias	The tendency to systematically under or over forecast. See MPE.
Biased Adjusted Mean Absolute Error (BAMAE)	An error metric that compensates for the tendency of traditional error metrics to reflect bias in an inconsistent manner, depending on the volatility of the data series.
Bucket	A unit of time used to measure actual or forecast values, e.g. a week or month
Business Forecasting	Medium term – usually financial - forecasts used to steer the performance of a business.
Causal Models	Forecasting algorithms based on the decomposition of history into different elements that are forecast separately before being recombined.
Cleaning (history)	The process of removing the impact of non-recurring events from historic data before applying a forecasting model
Coefficient of Variation (COV)	A measure of volatility. The standard deviation expressed as a percentage of mean demand.

Consensus Forecasting	A process whereby the contextual knowledge of different parties are judgementally combined to create an 'agreed' forecast.
Continuous Demand	A demand series where all data points have a positive value (see intermittent demand)
Cycle Stock	That part of an inventory that is required to meet the forecast demand. (see safety stock)
Data point	A value for a single bucket in a data series
Demand Sensing	A type of forecasting software that uses proprietary algorithms to adjust forecasts based on short term demand data.
Demand Series	A sequence of actual values for a variable
Discontinuity	The point at which the nature of the pattern of demand significantly changes
Expediting costs	The incremental cost of securing more product at short notice (within replenishment lead times)
Forecast	An estimate of expected future demand.
Forecast Accuracy (FA)	A measure of the accuracy of low level forecasts for a single period. Calculated by adding absolute low level errors, expressed as a deviation from zero errors (100% FA). Effectively FA is 100% less WAPE.

Forecast Cycle	The frequency at which forecasts are refreshed.
Forecast Error	The difference between actual demand and a given forecast for a given bucket.
Forecast Horizon	The entire period covered by a forecast
Forecast Lag	The number of buckets between when a forecast is made and the period that it refers to.
Forecast stability	The rate at which forecasts for a given bucket change between forecast cycles
Forecast Value Added (FVA)	A measure of how the accuracy of forecasts changes between different steps in the process. (see value added)
Forecastability	The ease of forecasting. A product of the complexity of the signal and the level of noise.
Intermittent Demand	A demand series where a significant number of data points have a value of zero.
Kanban	A replenishment process usually associated with lean manufacturing practice, whereby an item is replaced as soon as it is consumed (see simple replenishment)
Lumpy Demand	A demand series where a number of data points have significantly higher values that the majority.
Mean Absolute Percentage Error (MAPE)	A measure of the average size of forecast error. Calculated by taking the average absolute error (ignoring the direction) and dividing by either the actual or forecast demand.

Mean Percentage Error (MPE)	A measure of the direction of forecast error (bias). Calculated by taking the average error over a data range and dividing by either the total actual or forecast demand.
Model	A simplified (quantitative) representation of patterns of demand, usually derived by analysing data series
Naïve Forecast	A forecast based on the actual demand for a prior period – usually the previous one
Naïve Forecast Error	The different between the naïve forecast and the actual, used to measure the volatility of a demand AND (when compared to actual forecast error) to measure the impact of using a simple replenishment strategy.
Noise	That part of a demand series attributable to random perturbations which have no discernible cause or repeatable pattern, and so are unforecastable
One set of numbers	Using the same forecast numbers for operational and business forecasting purposes.
Operational Forecasting	Short term – usually non financial forecasts – that aim to improve the ability of the business to respond to demand.
Overfitting	The tendency of mathematical models to fit to noise, rather than to the signal in a data series, so leading to a degradation in forecast quality.

Relative Absolute Error (RAE)	The ratio of actual forecast error to the naïve forecast error. A measure of the value added by forecasting.
Replenishment Lead Time	The lag between a replenishment order on an (internal or external) supplier being generated and it being fulfilled.
Replenishment Order	An order placed on an (internal or external) supplier for the replenishment of stock.
Safety Stock	That part of inventory that is held to ensure that customer service can be maintained in the event that demand is under forecast. Calculated with reference to the variation in forecast error and the targeted service level.
Seasonality	Any repeated (cyclical) pattern of behaviour in a data series.
Signal	That part of a demand series that represents the 'true' level of demand, i.e. excluding noise.
Stationary demand	Where there is no trend or seasonality in the demand signal.
Stock Keeping Unit (SKU)	An item held for sale with a unique set of attributes. Typically, this is at a very low level in a product hierarchy and carries a code used for stock record and replenishment purposes.
Simple Replenishment	A replenishment strategy based on replacing items that have just been sold, rather than a forecast. See Kanban.
Standard Deviation	A measure of the volatility of a data series around its mean.

Statistical	Describing any method based on an analysis of probabilities.
Target	A quantitative expression of an aspiration (e.g. for a level of sales)
Time Series Models	Forecasting methods based on the statistical analysis of historical patterns of demand.
Unavoidable Error	That error that can be attributed to noise.
Value Added	Value is added whenever the actual forecast error is lower than the naïve error, since this measures the impact of adopting a simple replenishment strategy (i.e. not attempting to anticipate demand). See Relative Absolute Error.
Variable:	The thing being forecast. Usually assumed to be sales.
Variation	Unsystematic error, i.e. excluding bias. Partly attributable to noise.
Weighted Absolute Percentage Error (WAPE)	A measure of the accuracy of low level forecasts in a single period. Calculated by adding absolute low level errors, divided by the total actual demand in a period. See Forecast Accuracy.

CALCULATING VALUE ADDED METRICS

STEP 1: CALCULATE THE (BIAS ADJUSTED) ACTUAL ABSOLUTE ERROR

    1. Calculate bias: average net error (i.e. taking account of the sign – positive or negative)
    2. Calculate variation of each period: actual error less bias (then expressed as an absolute number – ignoring the sign)
    3. Calculate the mean variation: the sum of the period variation/number of periods
    4. Calculate the mean actual absolute error: variation plus absolute bias (i.e. ignoring the sign)

STEP 2: CALCULATE THE (BIAS ADJUSTED) NAÏVE ABSOLUTE ERROR

Calculate the naïve error: Actual for current period less actual for prior period

Repeat steps 1 – 4 using the naïve error.

STEP 3: CALCULATE THE (BIAS ADJUSTED) RELATIVE ABSOLUTE ERROR

How to calculate (Bias Adjusted) RAE

STEP 1 Calculate (Bias Adjusted) actual absolute error

① Calculate bias

	Period 1	Period 2	Period 3	Period 4	Period 5	Total	Average
Forecast	4	4	4	4	4	20	4.0
Actual	1	4	3	2	5	15	3.0
Bias	1	1	1	1	1	5	1.0
Variation	2	1	0	1	1	6	1.2
Mean Total Absolute Error							2.2

② Calculate variation for each period

③ Calculate mean variation

④ Calculate mean total (absolute error)

STEP 2 Calculate (Bias Adjusted) naive absolute error using the same method.

① Note: naive forecast for P2 = actual for P1 etc

	Period 1	Period 2	Period 3	Period 4	Period 5	Total	Average
Forecast		1	4	3	2	10	2.5
Actual	1	4	3	2	5	14	3.5
Bias		·1	·1	·1	·1	-4	-1.0
Variation		2	2	2	2	8	2.0
Mean Total Absolute Error							3.0

② Note: 4 period average only — no naive forecast for P1

STEP 3 Calculate (Bias Adjusted) RAE

$$2.2 / 3.0 = 0.73$$

RECOMMENDED READING

Mike Gilliland; The business forecasting deal: exposing myths, eliminating bad practices, providing practical solutions Wiley 2010
An easy to read guide for practitioners from a pragmatically minded expert and the inventor of Forecast Value Added. The first port of call for readers wanting to go to the next level

Stephan Kolassa, Enno Siemsen; Demand forecasting for managers, Business Expert Press 2016
A relatively straightforward overview of forecasting methods. A simple reference guide for those wanting to understand more about the mathematical basis of forecasting.

Mike Gilliland, Udo Slavo, Len Tashman: Business forecasting: practical problems and solutions, Wiley 2015
An edited collection of the most important articles, mainly culled from Foresight – the International Institute of Forecasters journal for practitioners. Read this to get a good grounding into the latest thinking.

Paul Goodwin; Forewarned: A Sceptics Guide to prediction, Biteback Publishing 2017
An overview of the practice of prediction and some of the pitfalls for the layman written by a recognised academic expert.

Philip Tetlock, Dan Gardner; Superforecasting: The Art and Science of Prediction, Random House 2015
A popular science book on the work of the most respected academic expert on forecasting expertise. Learn how foxes (non-experts with a questioning mind) outperform hedgehogs (experts blinkered to evidence).

Steve Morlidge; Future Ready: How to Master Business Forecasting, Wiley 2010
The only book written about medium term (mainly financial) forecasting for business practitioners.

STOP PRESS

JUST OUT!

... a buyers guide to forecasting methods and how they are implemented in software

Acknowledgements

Many of the lessons in this book are derived directly from my personal experience of working with clients and their data, but it would be remiss of me if I was not to acknowledge the enormous debt that I owe to other members of the global forecasting community. Without exception they have been unstintingly generous with their time and expertise as I have blundered around asking stupid questions, which, just occasionally, uncovered new insights in places where conventionally educated forecasters would not normally look.

I would like to thank Professor Paul Goodwin and Professor Aris Syntetos with whom I have worked directly. Many people at the acknowledged global centre of forecasting expertise at Lancaster University, UK, have also been very supportive. In particular I acknowledge a debt to Professor Robert Fildes who founded the Centre for Forecasting and Professor John Boylan, its current leader. I seek the forgiveness of all these – and many other - experts if, in my eagerness to help forecasters, I have unwittingly promoted ideas that make them feel slightly uncomfortable. Wherever I had to make a choice, I have chosen pragmatism based on personal experience of what works rather than technical rectitude, but the experts mentioned above are who you should seek out if you are looking for deep expertise.

In the USA, Mike Gilliland of SAS has unselfishly encouraged my efforts in many practical ways, as has Len Tashman, the irrepressible editor of Foresight Magazine, the practitioners' journal affiliated to the International Institute of Forecasting. I would also like to thank Anish Jain of the Institute for Business Forecasting for the platform he has given me to share my ideas.

I would never have started this book without enlightened practitioners who appreciated how the insights I have shared could be used to improve the value that they as forecasters could add to their businesses. In particular, I would like to thank David Hawes of Accolade Wines and Simon Clarke at Coca Cola. Also, Crispin Mair of Crimson Consulting has supported me in ways too numerous to mention.

Finally, thanks to Mike Hartley, my business partner at CatchBull who has indulged my unguided enthusiasm for all the challenges faced by forecasters, irrespective of whether it helps sell stuff, and Trevor Hilder and Nat James who have been brilliant in helping us translate our insights into working software.

ABOUT THE AUTHOR

Dr Steve Morlidge is married to Sue and has three grown children and a small white dog.

He is a management thinker, speaker, writer and founder of CatchBull Ltd, an innovator in forecast performance management software, mainly for the supply chain community.

He lives in the Surrey countryside, south of London.

If you want to buy multiple copies of this book for friends or colleagues, or if you are interested in creating a special customised edition of this book for your organisation, contact me at steve.morlidge@catchbull.com

I would welcome your comments and suggestions about this book - positive or negative.

This little book about forecasting comes with a big message for forecasters and their audience.

Most books in forecasting bury the important perspectives in methodological detail. This one stands above the forest: it offers so many memorable takeaways that you'd almost like to commit the text to memory. And Steve does all this with simplicity, style, and humor. It's quite an accomplishment.

Len Tashman, Editor of Foresight, the premier publication for business forecasters.

The essential forecasting primer for the first-time forecaster or practitioner wanting to know more. Excellence in forecasting stems from understanding more than algebra and the mechanical application of predictive analytics. An appreciation of the potential perils and pitfalls, low-yield activities and must-do's is crucial. I thoroughly recommend this book as a great introduction into themes that will elevate the knowledge and awareness of a forecaster in the field.

Simon Clarke, Group Director of Forecasting, The Coca-Cola Company

Very comprehensive and well-organized – touching on essential yet frequently overlooked elements of the business forecasting process. The book is arranged in bite-sized chunks, each delivering an important point, while the message is re-enforced by an accompanying graphic. Both practicing forecasters, and the managers who oversee or participate in the forecasting process, will find this a fast and invaluable read.

Michael Gilliland, Product Marketing Manager - SAS Forecasting. Author of 'The Forecasting Deal' and principal-editor of 'Business Forecasting: Practical Problems and Solutions'

A highly accessible and concise guide to practical forecasting presented in a style that is both informal and engaging. The author skilfully combines his broad experience of forecasting in commercial environments with the latest thinking in the field to distil important and valuable lessons that should lead to significant improvements in customer service and reduced inventory costs.

Paul Goodwin, Emeritus Professor Bath University. Author of Decision Analysis for Management Judgement, Forewarned: A Sceptics Guide to Prediction and Profit from Your Forecasting Software

Steve has an almost unique capability to make an at times mind-boggling subject interesting and fun! In this book, he describes techniques and makes observations that range in complexity from the simple to the sophisticated, providing something for forecasting practitioners of every level.

Crispin Mair, Director Crimson & Co, Supply Chan Consultants